DARE GREATLY

A High School Girl's Bible Study on
Thriving in Your Teens

DARE GREATLY

A High School Girl's Bible Study on
Thriving in Your Teens

HANNAH DUGGAN

CROSS
HILL
PRESS

ISBN-13: 978-0692648612
ISBN-10: 0692648615

Praise for Hannah Duggan

"Hannah is a wunderkind. A prodigy. She is an up-and-comer with remarkable talent."

-Pastor Ben Courson
Applegate Christian Fellowship

"I've read *From the Flames* & found it to be a fascinating read! I was not only extremely impressed, but equally blessed by Hannah's words. The Lord's hand is upon this young lady!"

-Pastor Mike Stangel
North Shore Christian Fellowship

"As a young woman Hannah has a way of connecting with girls where they are at and challenging them to a deeper maturity with each other and in their relationship with Jesus."

-SuperiorMom05
Amazon Reviewer

"Hannah's heart for girls seeps through the pages! *Just Us Girls* points each girl, regardless of her age or circumstances to Jesus, the Anchor of her soul."

-Kelsey Erich
Youth Leader
Calvary Chapel Honolulu

"As a senior pastor's wife I was able to see fresh ways to approach young ladies as I gained insights from Hannah. *Just Us Girls* offers big sisterly advice and practical road signs of what to expect ahead."

-Kathy Newman
Women's Ministry Leader
Calvary Chapel Windward

What Teen Girls Are Saying About *Dare Greatly*

"*Dare Greatly* covers everything from boys to stress to sharing your faith, and it's really inspired me to grow closer to God, to achieve His standards instead of anyone else's. In short, this is a teen girl's guide to attaining her God-given potential."

-Elizabeth Newsom, Age 17
Blogger

"I loved the whole book! It was so helpful and enjoyable. Always looking forward to Hannah's new books and Bible studies. Can't wait for more!"

-Evangeline, Age 14

"I really enjoyed *Dare Greatly*, and I thought it had a lot of great knowledge and things that I could easily apply to my own life."

-Claire, Age 16

"I adored a lot of things about *Dare Greatly*. My favorite part was that every chapter was connected to a real-life story or situation, which kept the chapters incredibly relatable. LOVED every moment of it!"

-Peyton, Age 14

"*Dare Greatly* shows us that there is so much more to being a Christian teenager. It shows us how to have faith, love, and to dare."

-Olivia, Age 14

"*Dare Greatly* is teaching us how to finally let go of our old selves and move on to reinvent ourselves in Christ. Thank you, Hannah!"

-Tierney, Age 13

Other Books by Hannah Duggan

Fiction

From the Flames: A Novel

Dear Kate: A Novel

Non-Fiction

Just Us Girls: A Bible Study on Being God's Girl in Middle School

Dare Greatly: A High School Girl's Bible Study on Thriving in Your Teens

For the girls
Studying on living room floors,
Circled up in sanctuaries,
And praying alone in your rooms.
You are a force to be reckoned with.
You inspire me.

Contents

INTRODUCTION

When I sat down to write this book I had it all figured out. I was going to write the Christian girl's guide to surviving high school. Then I stared at a blank computer screen for a few days and came to the conclusion that I was doing something wrong. After a lot of soul-searching, brain cudgeling, and desperate face-down prayer, I realized what it was: I was writing the wrong book.

I was writing a survival book for teen girls, but these girls wanted more than survival. As I emailed, skyped, and sat down with girls from all over the country, I saw that I wasn't giving them nearly enough credit. These girls are extraordinary! They're starting on-campus Bible studies. They have radical testimonies. They don't want to survive. They want to change the world.

These girls came at me with tough issues, deep theological concepts, and real-life problems. They wanted to know how to reach out to their unsaved friends. They wanted to know exactly what God says about finding their soul mate. In short, they wanted to know what God expects from them as young women.

I teared up reading their responses. They didn't want a book that simply addressed their issues. They were craving more than that. They wanted a challenge. They wanted a dare.

Instead of addressing ten issues, this book issues ten dares.

Dare Greatly is a glimpse into the victorious, spirit-filled life. We all want a life like that, but we consider it out of reach. God intended for us to live extraordinary lives! He gave us the powerful promises of His Word. Right now. Today. He created us to…

- ❀ Live our lives Exceptionally
- ❀ Wait for our future spouse Patiently
- ❀ Conquer our fears Courageously
- ❀ Adorn ourselves Valiantly
- ❀ Run this race of faith Dauntlessly
- ❀ Fight our spiritual battles Relentlessly
- ❀ Transform our lives Endlessly
- ❀ Trust our Lord Faithfully
- ❀ Go into this dark world Boldly
- ❀ Walk out our beliefs Confidently
- ❀ Dare Great things for the Kingdom of God

Throughout Paul's letters to the churches, we find one of his favorite Greek words. He used it so often that we find this word in almost every one of his letters. The word is *parakleo*. It means "to encourage, exhort, instruct, summon, or beseech." Sometimes it's translated "comfort." But it's not the squishy, pillowy comfort we think of. It's a form of encouragement from a teacher to a student or more specifically from a coach to an athlete. In essence, the word *parakleo* means "to dare." For example, in Romans 12:1 Paul says, "I *parakleo* you brethren, by the mercies of God that you present you bodies as a living sacrifice…" Paul was constantly daring the churches to live radical lives for Jesus Christ. *That* is the kind of study teens need in this day and age. In this generation we all fall into complacency. We need to be awakened. We need a challenge. We need *parakleo*.

Because I believe that these girls are capable of changing the world as we know it. They are bursting with dreams and God-given ideas. They need someone to look them in the eye and tell them, "You are God's extraordinary force on the earth. You were meant to defy every expectation and break every record. You were given a story to tell that no one else on the face of the earth is ever going to tell, and you do not have to do it alone."

Theodore Roosevelt said that it's not the critics that count, but the man who is actually in the arena, doing the work, "…*who at the best knows in the end the triumph of high achievement, and who at the worst, if he fails, at least fails while daring greatly…*"

What if we lived our lives like that? What if we could let go of our fear of failure? What if we dared to endeavor great things for God?

We don't have to wait one more day to conquer our

fears, find our joy, and live out God's will. He designed us to thrive, died a brutal death so that we could live an abundant life. Not tomorrow. Not next week. Not after you graduate. Right now.

Dare Greatly is more than just a poetic idea or a motivational quote. Consider this Bible study more than just a devotional. Consider it a dare. From one sister to another. I dare you, beloved. I dare you to dare greatly.

If you are a teen reading this Bible study...

This book has been designed to meet you right where you're at. If you picked up this book to read on your own, you and I are going to have a blast. Talking with girls is one of my favorite things on this earth. I talk with them through email, Skype, and social media, but my favorite way to connect with people is over a cup of coffee, face to face. Consider this our coffee date. In these pages you and I are going to get together once a week and dig into God's Word together. Then we're going to look at practical tools that challenge us to live out what we've learned.

I encourage you to do the daily devotionals. They don't take long, and whenever we spend some extra time in God's Word we will not be disappointed. However, if you don't have time to do the devotional, I encourage you to read the chapters and consider what they mean for you personally. We can read a lot of great Bible study books, but if they don't change the way we live, we're doing something wrong. God's Word isn't just meant to be read. It's meant to be applied.

One of the things I really want to drive home with this study is that you are not alone. If I've learned anything from writing Bible studies, it's that the Lord has an incredible network of teen girls all over the world. But so many of us feel isolated and lonely. My sisters, this thing ought not to be so! Firstly, I just want to say that hearing from you is one of my favorite things in the whole world. So often, the emails I get start with, "I'm so sorry for bothering you…" or "I know you're busy…"

Let me make something perfectly clear. You are the reason I do what I do. I want to connect with you. I want to hear from you. You inspire me. Don't ever hesitate to write me, because it will be the highlight of my day. You can find me on social media:

Instagram: @author_hannah_duggan
Twitter: @author_hannah_d
Facebook: www.facebook.com/hannahdugganauthor/
Pinterest: (I love it so.) @hannahduggan.94

You can also contact me through my website:
www.authorhannahduggan.wordpress.com

Or just shoot me an email:
authorhannahduggan@gmail.com

That's how you can find me, but I want you to be able to connect with each other as well. The Bible says that we are to encourage one another and build each other up (1 Thes. 5:11). Social media is one of the best ways we can do that over long distances. If you want to connect with others, post your favorite findings, treasures, and discoveries to social media using the hashtag

#DareGreatlyStudy

We were never meant to walk this journey of faith alone. We need to be active about connecting with one another. We need to encourage and challenge each other as we chase after God's heart.

One more thing! This book has been designed for you to *use* not just to read. There are spaces in the study guides where you can write your answers. Doodle in it! Dog ear it! Underline what speaks to you, and scribble your brilliant thoughts in the margins. This isn't the kind of book that remains in pristine condition on the shelf. This is your comfy, constant companion. Love it well.

If you are a Bible Study Leader...

First of all, thank you. Thank you so much for reaching out to the teen girls in your life and making an impact for the Kingdom. In high school what all of us need is an adult who really believes in us. You are that adult for these girls. Thank you for changing their lives so that they can change the lives of others.

You can find a multitude of resources on my website (www.authorhannahduggan.wordpress.com). Whether you're opening your home or giving up a night of your week, I've hopefully made your job a little easier. In the leader guide you'll find discussion questions that parallel the girls' homework. You'll also find fun ideas for activities and ice-breakers. You can download printables, like weekly memory verse cards and fun quotes to share with your girls. If you want to give your group an extra challenge, you can download the "Word of the Week" sheets. Each week, the girls can study one Greek or Hebrew word that will correlate with their Bible study homework and give them a deeper study experience.

As I said above, I love to connect with the girls. I've had the opportunity to Skype, FaceTime, and even come speak for different study groups. It is such a blast. I would love to do this for your Bible study. If you have any questions, send me an email at authorhannahduggan@gmail.com.

God has great things in store for you, whether you're a study group or an individual. I am praying that when we study the things He has for us in this book, we will walk away as different people. We will be the kind of young women who live more than "normal lives." We will be the kind of young women who know the triumph of high achievement. We will be young women who dare greatly.

CHAPTER 1

LIVE EXCEPTIONALLY

But the Lord said to me:
"Do not say, 'I am a youth,'
For you shall go to all to whom I send you,
And whatever I command you,
You shall speak."

JEREMIAH 1:7

Stepping Up

Taking the Dare

"I dare you!"

I studied the six-year-old specimen in front of me. His tennis shoes were planted firmly in the wood chips of the playground, his arms crossed, his beady eyes fixed on me. Being six-years-old myself, I failed to recognize that I had come face-to-face with a fantastic specimen of *Schola Probus*, more commonly known as "The School Bully." Plague of the playground, terror of kindergartners everywhere, this power-hungry tot was even accompanied by a gangly second-grade sidekick who didn't say much.

"I dare you!" he yelled again. "I dare you to lick the firetruck."

I examined the jungle-gym fashioned to look like a fire engine. Then I turned back to him. "Why?"

He gave me a look of pure *duh*. "Because I dared you."

I cocked my head, narrowing my gaze at him curiously. "But I don't care."

Needless to say, bullies never found me very entertaining and eventually gave up.

Someone recently told me that girls don't like to be dared. Given my own playground experience, I was inclined to agree. However, upon further consideration, I realized that girls don't mind a dare now and then. We like a challenge, something that we can strive for. We like a good dare. We just don't like a stupid dare (i.e. licking the famed firetruck of Helmen Elementary).

We're all called to do great things. We all have the ability to change the world, but sometimes the homework, the drama, and the stress of high school shove our big dreams to the back-burner.

In our teens it's so easy to feel like life is just beyond our reach. Teens love the word *someday*.

Someday I'll graduate high school.

Someday I'll have a fantastic career.

Someday I'll marry a wonderful man.

High school is a season of waiting, a season of someday.

Someday I'll figure out what I'm doing with my life.

Someday I'll find God's will.

Someday I'll do great things for God.

But what if I told you that we don't have to wait? What if we could do great things right now? What if it's not our age that need to change? What if it's our definition of "great things"?

Who You Really Are

When we think of "great things" we imagine things like curing cancer. That's a great goal, but the chances that you are going to accomplish that while you're in high school are pretty slim. Not impossible but slim. God might not be calling you to cure a deadly disease at the moment, but that doesn't mean He isn't calling you to do great things. God has a list of world-changing feats already prepared for you (Eph. 2:10), but I know that there are at least ten great things God is calling you to do right now because—what d'ya know—there are ten chapters in this book.

I have every confidence that the God that set planets in motion has a future and a hope for you. As Christian kids, most of us have all heard that before. We can recite Jeremiah 29:11. What we forget is that God doesn't just have a plan for our future, but also for our present.

Our age is such a great excuse to put God off.

When I was in high school I was reading in the Gospels about Jesus calling his disciples. They came from all walks of life, but they had one thing in common. When Jesus called, they dropped everything and followed Him without question. I remember coming to the realization that if Jesus called me to drop everything and follow Him, my answer would be, "Let me just finish my chemistry homework." (And I didn't even like chemistry!)

My question to you is this:

If Jesus asked you to drop everything and follow Him, what would stop you?

People's expectations?
The feeling that you're not good enough?
Fear of failure?
I'm not saying that the Lord wants you to drop out of

high school or sell all of your worldly possessions, but is He the most important thing in your life? If He *did* call you out of comfort zone, would you go?

Day after day we get weighed down, stressed out, and angry because of the overwhelming nature of our lives. But maybe it's not our lives that need to change. Maybe it's us. Maybe it's our mindset. Because no matter what our lives are like, we were all called to live them victoriously.

In our culture teens are expected to be stressed out. They're expected to be depressed. But I know how much you're capable of. I know because I see you almost every day.

You're in my social media feed.

You send me emails that make my day.

I've sat across from you in coffee shops.

I've seen you dance to the radio.

I've listened to you sob on the other end of the phone.

I'm endlessly dazzled by your sense of humor and awed by your courage.

It breaks my heart that so many people in this world don't understand you. They don't see the struggles that you face. They forget that high school is one of the hardest times of any girl's life. I know you've been labeled and looked down on just because of your age.

You are surrounded by people who have endless opinions on how you should live your life.

You can't escape the feeling that everyone is watching you, waiting to see if you'll fail at this whole "life" thing.

I know because I fight those same battles.

I've criticized my reflection, envied the girls who seemed to get away with everything, and cried myself to sleep at night because I didn't have a boyfriend. (Gurl, I been there.)

This world will tell you that you're not smart enough, pretty enough, or significant enough to make a difference. But I am telling you that your God wants you right now, just as you are! Because the world might look at us and see someone worth passing over, but do you know what I see when I look at you?

I see passion that has been dampened by precaution.

I see faith that has been choked out by fear.

I see dreams that are treading the waters of your doubt.

I see the warrior inside you.

I see the scars you try to hide, and I know that God can use them to transform the lives of others.

I see the spark of the Divine in your incredible mind.

I see the struggling flicker of hope that the world has tried to suffocate.

When I look at you, I see God's game-changer.

Buckling Down

You are a powerful force, and it is time to stop believing that you are a mediocre girl meant for mediocre things.

You are exceptional.

And yes, you struggle. You doubt. You make mistakes, but your God has a passion so deep for you that it conquered Hell.

He did *not* create you to live in depression.

He did *not* create you to live in fear.

He wants you to live a life of joy and peace no matter what you are going through.

That is what this book is for. To teach us how we can live that kind of life right now. How to walk in victory instead of defeat. How we can live each day as a child of the God who rose from the dead.

Because this life is a battle that's been rigged for your victory, but living that kind of life doesn't happen by accident. It takes work.

In the book of Exodus God rescued the children of Israel from captivity in Egypt. Deliverance was His gift to them just as salvation is His gift to us. He saved us from Satan just like He saved them from Pharaoh. But because of their fear and doubt, the Israelites didn't get to dwell in the Promised Land. God had parted the Red Sea for them, and they still wouldn't dare to believe in His power. So they wandered in the desert for forty years. Oh sure, they'd been "delivered." They weren't slaves anymore. They were saved, but they were miserable. And you and I can be saved, redeemed, good little Christian girls and still be completely miserable if we don't dare to believe in the power of our God. The Promised Land was Israel's for the taking, but if they wanted to live the life of blessing that God intended for them, they had to take it back from an army of giants. Jesus told us that He came so we could have more abundantly (John 10:10).

Over the next ten weeks we're going to take back our Promised Land. It's going to take work, but that's why the title of this book isn't *Dare Averagely*.

"Faith can move mountains,
but don't be surprised if God hands you
a shovel."
-Unknown

That is the purpose of this study. I want to dig into God's Word with you, because no matter what you're facing, the answer is in there. Teens are becoming a group known for being self-centered and depressed. We have the opportunity to be the exception.

If we truly understand God's love for us and His work on the cross, we can speak light into the darkness and stare down our greatest fears. You weren't meant to just survive this season of your life. You were meant to live exceptionally.

CHAPTER 1

LIVE EXCEPTIONALLY

DAILY STUDY GUIDE

Day 1
Read Jeremiah 1:4-10

What is God calling Jeremiah to do?

Why doesn't he want to do it?

What does God think of Jeremiah's excuse?

What gift does God give Jeremiah?

Has God ever asked you to do something that sounded crazy? What was it?

Why were you/are you afraid to do it? Are you going to let that fear stop you?

This is one of my favorite passages of Scripture. I come back to it whenever I'm overwhelmed or discouraged. We all need to be reminded that God knows exactly who we are even if we don't, and He has called us to do great things anyway. My favorite part about this passage is that it's a conversation. It isn't a one-sided discussion of Jeremiah whining to the Lord. As hesitant as he was to follow through, Jeremiah still let the Lord speak to him. Often, we pour out our wants and needs and don't let the Lord get a word in edge-wise. If we're going to live exceptionally, we need to communicate with our exceptional God. Your first dare is to have a consistent devotion time. It doesn't have to take long. I know high school is busy, but my mom always said that if you have time to feed yourself physically, you have time to feed yourself spiritually. First, you speak to God. It's always helped me to write my prayers, but maybe verbal prayer is easier for you. Lay your plans, worries, and needs before Him. If you have any decisions you need to make, now is the time to ask Him. Then let God speak to you. It doesn't have to be a burning bush or a booming voice. Open His Word and read what it has to say. He will meet you there. I promise.

Day 2
Read Philippians 4:4-7

There are four commands from God in this passage (five if you count the repeated one). What are they?

🌸

🌸

🌸

🌸

What promise follows these commands?

The amazing thing about these commands is that there are no conditions. None of them are tagged with "when you feel like it" or "just around some people." All of these commands are characterized by absolute words.

🌸 *Always*
🌸 *To all men*
🌸 *For Nothing*
🌸 *In Everything*

These are "once-and-for-all" kind of commands. When is it hardest to obey them?

Which of these commands is the hardest for you to obey?

All of us have a hard time with these commands, but some of us struggle in different areas. Some of us are easily depressed and have a hard time being joyful. Some of us tend toward worry and anxiety. But here's the cool thing about this passage: If God commands it of us, it's possible. So often, we let our feelings cloud our judgment. We say thing like, "I can't help it. It's just the way I feel." But here God orders us to take control of our mind and of our feelings. Best of all, He tells us how to do it. "…by prayer and supplication, with thanksgiving, make your requests be made known to God." When we bottle up our concerns and feelings, they get ugly. It's hard to live an exceptional life when you're an emotional wreck. Trust me. I've tried. The key is to lay our concerns at His feet, believing that He knows best. Then we need to leave our worries there and trust Him to deal with them. When you do that, "the peace of God will guard your hearts and minds through Christ Jesus." Those aren't just pretty words. That is a promise from God to you. So don't wait another second. Pour out your heart to Him in the space below, and let His peace stand guard over you heart and mind.

Day 3
Read Deuteronomy 1:28-33

Who is speaking?

Who is he speaking to?

Why didn't Israel want to enter the Promised Land?

What was God's promise to them? Did they heed it?

God was calling Israel to live exceptionally in the land He'd promised them. In their moment of fear, what did Moses remind them of?

Describe a time when the Lord fought for you or carried you through.

The heartbreaking thing about this passage is verse 32. "Yet, for all that, you did not believe the Lord your God." If anyone had witnessed miracles, it was the children of Israel. God went before them, protected them, and provided for them in the desert. They got to see God in ways you and I don't. Every day He led them as a pillar of cloud, at night a pillar of fire. But when push came to shove, they forgot how big their God was. And you and I can do the exact same thing. When God calls us to live exceptional lives, we forget everything He's already done for us. Below, write down a time when the Lord protected you from something you couldn't see, provided for you, or showed you His mighty power.

DAY 4
Read Hebrews 4:1, 11-13

What promise remains for us?

What *should* we fear?

What should we be diligent about? Why?

According to verse 12, how do we enter into this promise?

If you look back at the end Hebrews 3, you'll see that the writer was just discussing the children of Israel wandering through the desert who never entered God's rest. What do you think it means that God has promised us rest? How is it different from the rest He promised Israel?

These chapters use words like "disobedience" and "rebellion." We usually equate these words to "bigger" sins. Why do you think rest is such a big deal to God?

Your challenge today is to find areas of stress in your life that you need to confess, places in your heart that you are holding back from God. We all have them. It's painful, but when we repent we can be forgiven and freed. When we give those areas of stress to Him, He is finally able to heal us and give us the courage we need.

DAY 5
Read John 10:9-11

What is Jesus' first title in this passage?

What promise goes along with this title?

What is a thief's job description?

What is Jesus' second title in this passage?

The thief Jesus is talking about is the enemy. How has the enemy tried to steal, kill, and destroy in other people's lives?

What has he tried to steal from you?

What good things has he tried to kill?

How has he tried to destroy you?

Why didn't he succeed?

Okay, so the two titles might seem kind of random to us, but in that day they were very connected. It was a shepherd's job to guard the sheep. The pen where they would keep the sheep didn't have a very strong gate. So at night the shepherd would lay down at the entrance to protect the flock. Therefore Jesus is both our Shepherd and our Door. The life he describes here is one of safety and freedom. When sheep are with their master, they are content. They're not constantly worrying about their shepherd's skills and qualifications. They trust Him for their every need, and He delivers. Yet we don't live like that with the God of our salvation. The biggest key to living an exceptional life is trusting the Lord, handing everything over to Him, and not worrying about tomorrow. Today, find specific situations in your life that you have to trust Him for. Below, thank Him that He's got it under control. It's when we start trusting our Shepherd that our lives become both abundant and exceptional.

CHAPTER 2

WAIT PATIENTLY

It is good that one should hope
And wait quietly
For the salvation of the Lord.

LAMENTATIONS 3:26

What to Do About the Boys

The Elusive Happy Ending

I had completely lost myself in the chick-flick.

I had reached the glorious finale of *Anne of Green Gables*. The sun was setting over Avonlea. Anne's hero was coming over the horizon. After a touching conversation, he reached out and twisted a strand of her red hair, his voice softening as he teasingly called her *Carrots*. One couldn't help but sigh with satisfaction as they walked back over the sun-streamed hills toward their happy ending. It was a perfect, breathtaking moment. Until I was snapped back to reality.

I was crammed in a living room with a dozen other teen girls. We were squished together on couches and blow-up mattresses.

"Oh my gosh!" one of the girls sobbed around a mouthful of chocolate. "Dat ish sho ro*man*tic!"

I looked around the room at the less-than-romantic view. Everyone looked somewhat bedraggled. None of us had showered. We had consumed unholy amounts of sugar. We all looked like trolls, huddled around the TV, chocolate staining our faces, candy wrappers stuck in our hair. I couldn't help but laugh. Because no matter who we are, what we hope to get out of life, or what time of the month it is, we can all use a little romance.

Let's face it, we all love a good happy ending. We all hope to have one ourselves someday. We live in a world where more than half the marriages end in divorce. Heartbreak and disappointment seem almost inescapable. There are plenty of people out there who honestly believe that the happy ending we're searching for is unattainable. But it just so happens that my God has a knack for happy endings, and when He wrote His Word, He didn't forget us hopeless romantics.

It's Kind of a Big Deal

I was recently waiting to pick up my brother in the high school parking lot. A few teens nearby were having a loud discussion, and I heard the words "God," "Jesus," and "Bible." I soon recognized that a young man was sharing his faith with a friend and couldn't help but smile. Then I heard their conversation.

Kid 1: "See, the Old Testament is a bunch of rules we don't have to follow anymore."

Me: *Mentally approves.* *We are no longer slaves of the law. Uh-huh. I'm tracking.*

Kid 1: "There's a lot of rules like...um...like..."

Me: *Mentally fills in blanks.* *"Don't eat pigs." "Wear four tassels." "Don't eat shellfish."*

Kid 1: "...like don't sleep with your brother's wife."

Me: *Mentally taps breaks.* *Hang on. What?*

Kid 1: "I mean, it's probably a good guideline. You can see how that would cause a lot of tension in the family dynamic, but it's not like we have to listen to any of those rules.

Me: *Fights impulse to run screaming across parking lot.* *What are you doing?! That's not what it means at all. Don't listen to him!*

There's probably an apology in order to Kid 1, whoever he is. I know he had good intentions, but it's sad how many Christians think like that. True, we are no longer under the law. Technically we don't *have to* follow God's laws for our lives, but we don't *have* to follow the manual for our car either. But have you ever seen what happens when you ignore the guidelines? A friend of mine once put regular gasoline in a diesel truck. It corroded from the inside out. By the time he got home, it was ruined.

God won't force us to follow His rules, but when He says something is a big deal, we need to take it seriously. Otherwise, we'll corrode and slowly tear ourselves apart from the inside out. So what does God have to say about love? Well, there are only a few "don'ts," but they're a pretty big deal.

Throughout the Bible there are only a few times we're told, "This is the will of God." And one of them can be found in Paul's letter to the Thessalonians.

> *For this is the will of God, your sanctification:*
> *That you abstain from sexual immorality.*

1 Thessalonians 4:3

This might seem basic, but it's amazing how Satan is lying to Christians in this generation. God says it again and again in His Word. There is no such thing as "safe sex" outside of marriage. It's only going to weigh us down and bring us heartbreak. While many of us might look at this verse and think, "I would never," Jesus told us in Matthew 5:28 that in God's eyes that sin begins in our mind. We need to guard our thoughts, because it is very possible to be squeaky clean on the outside, and a wreck on the inside.

The next thing that God makes a big deal about is something that is often overlooked, but is so important.

Do not be unequally yoked together with unbelievers.
For what fellowship has righteousness with lawlessness?
And what communion has light with darkness?

2 Corinthians 6:14

Non-believers are off-limits. Once again, this might sound harsh, but it is for our own good. So many sweet Christian girls have been dragged down dark paths by compromising what they believe. "Missionary Dating" (dating someone so they'll get saved) is so dangerous and can end up in an uneven, miserable marriage. Besides, as Christian young women, we need a man who can lead us closer to the Lord. We need someone we can pray with, someone who will fight back to back with us in our spiritual battles. It's never a good idea to go into a relationship to change someone. We can't change people. That's God's job.

Every Girl's Dream

What do you look for in a guy?

Tall, dark, and handsome? Strong and silent? Artistic? Athletic? If you're a girl between the ages of twelve and twenty, you've probably have had this conversation with your friends.

First, let me say that there is a line that shouldn't be crossed in these conversations. We can get carried away and wander from the daydream into the unhealthy, inappropriate, or discontent. But when we are sure to set a guard over our tongues, it's fun to daydream and joke about the guy God has picked for you.

Every girl should have two lists: a list of musts and a list of hopes.

The list of musts is the serious list, the one that doesn't change. The things that are on my list of musts are things like,

He *must* be a Christian.

He *must* love the Lord more than he loves me.

He *must* be a strong leader, someone I can trust and am willing to follow.

He *must* be able to handle my crazy, fun-loving family.

Then I have my list of hopes. These aren't deal-breakers but things I would like to see in a soul mate.

I *hope* he loves kids.

I *hope* he wants to spend his life in the ministry.

I *hope* he loves Marvel movies as much as me.

And I really *hope* he knows how to build bookshelves.

(I wouldn't exactly complain if he was good-looking either.)

Creating your list of musts and your list of hopes gives you so much clear direction. When you know what's important you're less likely to be distracted. You want a guy that meets your lists of musts, and if he doesn't, don't waste your time. It's not fair to you or to him.

Don't make your list of musts impossible.

It's all too easy to be searching for a "perfect guy"
instead of a guy who is perfect for you.

On the other hand, I've seen way too many girls who think that they're not pretty enough, smart enough, or skinny enough to wait for the right guy. So they settle for anyone who will take them.

Now maybe you've already met someone. Even if you're already in a relationship, I encourage you to make your lists. Sometimes we don't realize what's important to us until we put it on paper. And a girl should know what she wants.

Focusing on the Now

We're all waiting for something. Some of us are waiting for God to bring us our fella. Some of us are waiting for God to give us clear direction in our current relationship. However, while the Bible doesn't put an age limit on love, it does tell us to submit to godly authority. For most of us that's probably our parents. It's not only required of us as Christian young people (1 Pet. 5:5), it's healthy, and it's safe. All of us need that accountability, someone we can go to with our problems and concerns who can give us practical advice.

If you are in a relationship, I encourage you to ask yourself why. If the answer is that you love to be around him and he draws you closer to the Lord, there's nothing wrong with that. But we need to examine our hearts constantly. We need to make sure that we're not just with someone because it's convenient, because it's expected, or because we want to say that we have a boyfriend.

If you are not in a relationship, don't freak out. God's got the perfect guy for you. Take it from someone who is still waiting. This is a precious season in your life, and one you won't get to enjoy again. If you don't have a boyfriend, you're not a freak. It just means that God is giving you this time to focus on other areas of your life.

You were meant to live an adventurous life.
You need to find someone who makes that adventure even better.
Don't settle for anything less.

If you haven't met that person yet, then draw closer to your Savior every day and pray that He will continue to shape you into the woman that that godly man is waiting for. Regardless of where you're at, high school is a season of waiting, and that's okay. Hebrews 13:5 tells us not to covet what we don't have. We need to be content with what God has given us right now, knowing that our loving God is never going to forsake us.

He has a beautiful future and a breathtaking love story ahead of you. But don't rush ahead of Him.

It is good that one should hope
And wait quietly
For the salvation of the Lord.

Lamentations 3:26

God's got this one, beloved. Trust your Savior, and wait patiently.

CHAPTER 2

WAIT PATIENTLY

DAILY STUDY GUIDE

DAY 1
Read Lamentations 3:22-27

Why aren't we consumed?

Why do we hope in the Lord according to verse 24?

What are we to wait for?

When are we meant to bear the yoke?

This passage calls the Lord our portion. The Hebrew word for portion is *cheleq*. It means award, possession, or portion of land. At first glance, this verse means that the Lord is all we need in life. But *cheleq* has another definition. It also means flattery. Sometimes we don't even want a relationship with a guy as much as we want the flattery of his attention. We love it when someone is interested in us or gives us a second look. It makes us feel attractive and flattered. But the Lord sees even those petty desires in our heart. And yes, He is our portion, but He also satisfied our lesser needs. Because the unhindered love of God is all the flattery we need. Describe a time when God showed you that He was all you needed.

This passage is beautiful and almost poetic, and because of that we sometimes read right over the top of it. To really understand this passage, rewrite it in your own words. (Be ready to share this with your group.)

DAY 2
Read John 12:1-8

Where was Jesus?

What other familiar faces were at the dinner?

What did Mary do?

Who discouraged her?

What was Jesus' reaction?

Have you ever been mocked for a moment of worship or sacrifice? Was it still worth it? Explain.

This passage says a lot about worship, but what gets lost in translation is that it is also about love. That alabaster box that Mary broke was more than just perfume. It was most likely the most precious thing she owned, and more importantly, it was probably her dowry. Without it, she had little to no chance of getting married. By breaking it at Jesus' feet, she was saying, "I will trade in my future to worship You." That is commitment. Take a moment of worship. Spend some time with the Lord. Turn on some worship music if you like, and picture yourself in this scene. Take this time to give your love life to Him.

Day 3
Read 1 Peter 5:5-11

Who are these verses written to?

How many times does this passage tell us to "submit" or "be humble"?

Why are we supposed to be sober and vigilant, according to verse 8?

What four things will God do for us after we have suffered a while?

❁

❁

❁

❁

Humility can be hard to swallow. As young people, we see how different the world is from when our parents were kids, and it's easy to think that they can't understand what we go through. But the truth is, human nature hasn't changed at all, and they understand more than you think. We need to make sure—especially when it comes to romance—that we have accountability (someone who will check in with us to make sure we don't fall into temptation). Who is your accountability? Do they know it?

When the Bible says to be sober, it means that we need to be clear-headed. Our enemy is out for us, and he has used romance to take out more than one of your sisterhood in this world. We can't forget that we need to remain tuned in to God's voice above any other. While this season of waiting might be difficult, God has us here for a reason. List ways that this season of waiting has

❀ *Perfected You* —

❀ *Established You* —

❀ *Strengthened You* —

❀ *Settled You* —

Below, write a prayer, casting your cares upon Him, and thank Him for this season of your life.

DAY 4
Read Hebrews 13:5-6

What are we to be without?

Why are we told to be content?

What can we boldly say?

On a scale of 1 to *Get-Me-Out-Of-Here-I-Can't-Take-It-Anymore!!!* how content are you?

The Greek word for content is *arkeo*. It means to be "possessed with unfailing strength." I don't know about you, but that's not what I picture when I think of contentment. I've always thought of contentment as more of a non-feeling. When you're not feeling whiny, that's when your content, right? But Biblical contentment is an active fight. It also means "to defend or ward off." In other words, we have to fight for our contentment. What are three practical ways we can fight to be content?

❀

❀

❀

High school is one of the hardest seasons of life to be content, especially as we near graduation, but this passage contains a beautiful promise. Our Lord will never leave us or forsake us. Even when we feel our loneliest, we're not alone. Mankind isn't going to make or break us. Pray that the Lord will show you where you lack contentment. Write what He reveals to you below.

Day 5
Read John 15:9-17

What does Jesus command us to do twice in this passage?

Why did Jesus tell us these things?

Why did He choose us?

It's hard to try to wrap our minds around the idea of Jesus loving us the same way God the Father loves Him. Imagine that God's love is like the sky. It's vast and bigger than we can understand, and it's constantly pouring into the ocean, just like God's love pours into the Son. Jesus' love is like the ocean, also vast and able to contain the Father's love as well as return it back to him. Then there's us. We're like the little plastic cup that gets thrown away after parties. We can't touch the sky just like we can't touch the Father's love. The only way we can understand it is by seeing how the ocean reflects the sky. So when Jesus says He loves us, it's like trying to cram an entire ocean into a cup. That's how much Jesus loves us. Yet He asks us to abide in His love. To abide means to remain, endure, or survive. In other words, we are meant to survive on God's Love. How has God's love sustained you in this season of your life?

The Lord has such a passionate love for you. We've talk a lot this week about contentment, but we are not created to settle for less than God has for us. When it comes to romance, we need to know what we want in a husband. This week's dare: Create your list of musts and your list of hopes below.

CHAPTER 3

CONQUER COURAGEOUSLY

There is no fear in love;
But perfect love casts out fear,
Because fear involves torment.
But he who fears
Has not been made perfect in love.

1 JOHN 4:18

Overcoming Fear

Why Am I so Stressed?!

I'm behind schedule.

I haven't sent those emails yet.

I forgot to text my boss back.

I overslept.

Remember that commitment I made to exercise every morning? That sure went out the window fast.

Why does my room always look like the library threw up in it?

I really need to write back that friend. She dropped me a note...three weeks ago? She probably thinks I fell off the face of the earth or that I hate her or that I'm avoiding her. She probably doesn't even want to hear from me now. That's sad. I liked her.

"Would you mind working a few extra days this week?" Umm. Maybe I can squeeze that in between worship practice and feeding the neighbors cats.

Oh, that's right. One of the cats wouldn't come inside last night. What if something happened to the cat? What would I do? Do I text the neighbors? Or do I just wait until they get home? "Hi. How was Disneyland? Your cat died. Bye."

We've all felt that feeling of failure.

As teens, we're subjected to a lot of stressful situations that we can't avoid. Adults are told to "eliminate stress" in their lives and "remove themselves from stressful situations." But very few adults would approve if you planned to "eliminate homework" or "remove yourself from family gatherings."

As young adults, we often don't have a choice in the things that stress us out. So we ignore them. The longer we ignore it the uglier it gets. Before we know it, our days are filled with dread and our nights leave us wide-awake with anxiety.

Recently, I found myself on a Skype call with some beloved girls. I mentioned that I was starting a new Bible study and asked them what they would like to see in it.

"Would you do a chapter on stress and anxiety?"

I smiled. It just so happens I have a lot of experience being anxious and stressed. I need this chapter as much as you do.

The Lord is my Shepherd

Who knows the twenty-third Psalm? If you haven't read it or if you need a refresher, go look it up. It's one of the most famous passages of Scripture.

But what would the twenty-third Psalm look like if our lives were based in stress instead of trust?

The Lord is my Shepherd, but I just want to get this work done.
He keeps calling me to lie down in green pastures. What a great
metaphor.
Sadly, a walk beside the still waters doesn't fit into my schedule right
now.
One of these days life will slow down enough, and I'll let Him restore
my soul.
But right now, I need to walk this path of busyness for my name's
sake.
Yay. Another walk through the valley of the shadow of death.
Just what I need right now: the fear of evil.
God, I want to believe You're with me.
But all I can feel are Your rod and Your staff prodding me,
Like I'm in trouble or something.
Why do I keep ending up at a table full of my enemies?
Why does it feel like my life is constantly overflowing?
Surely stress and anxiety shall follow me all the days of my life.
And I will dwell in a house full of discouragement.
Forever.

Psalm 23 encapsulates every fear, every stress, and every source of human anxiety.

1. Decision making.

The Lord is my Shepherd…

I don't know about you, but one of my worst fears is that I'll miss God's will for my life. If we believe that the Lord is our Shepherd, all we have to do is follow Him. It's not easy, but it is simple. Did you know that shepherds never chase their sheep from behind or force them into something? They walk out in front, letting the sheep follow the sound of their voice.

Here's the great promise in this verse: If we believe that the Lord is our Shepherd, we're not going to get off course.

If we really believe He's got it figured out, He's not going to let us wander. If our lives are fully submitted to Him and we truly want His will, He won't let us stray.

2. Material needs.

I shall not want…

When I was a little kid, I misunderstood Psalm 23:1. I thought it said, "The Lord is the Shepherd I shall not want." *Wait. I thought we* did *want Him to be our Shepherd.*

Jesus instructed us in Matthew 6:31, "Therefore do not worry saying, 'What shall we eat?' or 'What shall we drink?' or 'What shall we wear?'" (That last one hits home, doesn't it?)

The second half of Psalm 23:1 depends on the first half. It's only when we believe the Lord is our Shepherd that we can trust Him with our needs.

When we're following the Lord,
He's going to provide for us.
Every. Single. Time.

---

3. Chaos.

He makes me to lie down in green pastures; He leads me beside the still waters.

"I just don't have time to read my Bible." I hear it all the time, sometimes coming out of my own mouth.

The Lord's invited us to rest, but if we wait for life to slow down before we accept the invite, we never will. And that's exactly how the enemy wants it. God doesn't just *ask* us to slow down and hand Him our worries in the midst of the chaos, He commands it. If we don't obey, the chaos is going to overwhelm us.

4. Sin.

He restores my soul...

At first glance, this sounds just like the last verse, but conditional. *If* we allow Him to lead us into green pastures beside still waters, *then* He is able to restore our soul. The Hebrew word for "restore" doesn't mean "rejuvenate" or "relax." It means to turn 180 degrees, completely changing your purpose and direction. A more literal translations would be, "He overhauls my soul."

Am I the only one who needs that? Most days I need more than just a tune up. I don't want the Lord to simply change the oil and check the coolant and top off the gas tank. I need an overhaul. I need Him to get a hold of my soul and turn me around before I wreck. But if I never walk beside the still waters, I'll never ever know my need, and He won't be able to work in me.

5. What will they think of me?

He leads me in the paths of righteousness for His name's sake.

I don't know about you, but I'm constantly afraid of what people think of me. Keeping up our name and our reputation is important to us. How many things do we do on a daily basis "for our name's sake"? Sometimes we'll even make life-changing decisions based on people's opinion of us. As a born perfectionist, I've found that much of my anxiety is caused by the fear that I will fail someone, but our name isn't the one that matters. Once we let go of our reputation, it's so much easier to follow God in paths of righteousness for *His name's sake.*

6. Death.

Yea, though I walk through the valley of the shadow of death…

As young people, we don't like to think about death. At best, we're okay with the fact that someday we're going to die. Not now. Later. Way down the road after we've lived a long, full life. But when we get that phone call, lose that loved one, walk through that trial, it's so hard to remember God is good. We can spend our lives terrified of what could go wrong and what we could lose, but there is beautiful promise in this Psalm. If we're allowing our Shepherd to lead us and restore us, we can overcome anything. I have seen people walk through horrible valleys and come out the other side victorious and in love with Jesus Christ. Hebrews 4:15 tells us that we have a High Priest who can sympathize with our weaknesses. Jesus cried at the tomb of His friend Lazarus. He understands loss and will walk us through those valleys.

7. Evil.

I will fear no evil; for You are with me…

There is plenty of evil to be feared in this world. We get a glimpse of it every time the news headlines a school shooting, a suicide bomber annihilates innocents, or ISIS beheads another victim. Those are very real, very terrifying circumstances, but none of them are stronger than our

God. Jesus never danced around the truth. He told us about the darkness. In John 16:33 He said, "These things I have spoken to you, that in Me you may have peace. In the world you will have tribulation; but be of good cheer, I have overcome the world."

There is a lie in our culture that says evil is simply misunderstood. On this subject James 1:16 tells us, "Do not be deceived, my beloved brethren." So many of us live in the fear of evil because we don't know how it works, but it's a series of choices. I mention this because it messed with me as a kid. I watched people I had grown up with go off the deep end of sin, and it scared me. I wondered how one earth they ended up there and had to learn that it was a result of their choices. Do not be deceived! Every one of us has been given a choice, and none of us have to choose the fear of evil.

8. Punishment

Your rod and Your staff, they comfort me.

1 John 4:18 lays it out clearly. "Perfect love casts out fear, because fear has to do with torment." There is a belief in some Christian circles that says if you are suffering, God is punishing you. That is a lie from the pit of Hell. Jesus Himself suffered. Are there natural consequences for our sin? Yes. But our God is "slow to anger, and abounding in mercy," (Ps. 103:8). When the devil is after us, reminding us of everything we've done, his accusations (while often true) are characterized by shame and guilt. When God corrects our hearts, even if the correction is painful, we will be overwhelmed by His great love. Just like the sheep that receives that gentle love tap

from the Shepherd's staff, we don't need to fear the comfort of His correction.

9. Enemies.

You prepare a table before me in the presence of my enemies…

When was the last time you found yourself at a table with your enemies? Was it the family reunion? The cafeteria? The dinner table? Here's what's crazy about this verse: It's listed as a blessing. Trust me, we all have our enemies. But the last time I came eye to eye with an enemy over a bowl of stale tortilla chips, I wasn't exactly pouring out the thanksgivings of my heart. It was awkward and scary. David knew all about awkward relationships. He was pals with King Saul…that is, at least before Saul tried to kill him. Not to mention he was best friends with Saul's son and—oh yeah—married to his daughter. David had no choice but to be faced with the awkward enemy factor over and over. Yet here he thanks God for it. I find it so interesting that a man of war like David would thank God, not for the defeat of his enemies, but for peace between them.

10. Destiny.

You anoint my head with oil…

David was anointed to be King even before he killed Goliath. Scholars estimate he was between the ages of 13 and 17. That's when he was chosen to be the king of Israel. No pressure! David wasn't trying to be the next king. He hadn't even finished high school (or whatever it was they had in Bethlehem), but that didn't stop God. God chose and anointed him while he was a youth. In the same way, God can call us to serve Him wherever, whenever He wants. Why is this frightening?

> ## The truth is, we're scared to death of who God wants us to be and what He could do through us.

He might be our Shepherd. He might have walked us through the valleys in our lives, but we're not quite willing to believe that He could use us. We can't live our lives in fear of God's anointing. It *is* scary. If we understand Him, it should be. His calling is always beyond us, but if He's called us to it, He's equipped us to do it.

11. Busyness.

My cup runs over.

"I have had it up to *here*."

When was the last time you felt that way? For me, it was fifteen minutes ago. We constantly feel like we're falling behind. Then we get irritated at our busy life. Then we feel guilty for being irritated. "My cup runneth over" sounds so poetic. In real life it looks a lot more like me hiding in the closet, binging on Netflix instead of facing my problems. We were meant to live full lives, overflowing with blessing. So why do blessings equal stress? The answer is in this verse. Our cup is meant to run over. But cups aren't nearly as popular in our culture as they were in ancient Israel. We prefer bottles (or Hydro Flasks!). Air-tight, sealed from all harm, made to last throughout the zombie apocalypse—the bottle containing the carbonated beverage only has one tiny flaw. It can't handle pressure. Shake that thing up, and you're bound to set it off. We were never meant to live lives like that. If we've "had it up to *here*" then something is wrong. We're not supposed to be topped off by pressure. We were meant to overflow with blessing, which means we have to let go of the things we can't control.

12. The Promise.

Surely goodness and mercy shall follow me all the days of my life; and I will dwell in the house of the Lord forever.

But wait! There's more. When we truly trust in God's faithfulness, goodness and mercy shall follow us. The Hebrew word for follow is *radaph*. It's literally translated, "to pursue, chase, and run after." Sister, if you are trusting the Lord, you won't be able to escape goodness and mercy all the days of your life. Sorry. You're stuck with 'em. You'll have to make your peace with the fact that "blessing will come upon you and overtake you," (Deut. 28:2). Our physical circumstances may change, but that's what is so amazing about our God. He is still God in the valley of the shadow of death. When we place our trust in Him, we are part of His family, and we will dwell in His house forever and ever and ever. As we follow our Shepherd, it doesn't matter what comes our way. We will dwell in the house of the Lord, overflowing with blessing, and when fear threatens us we will conquer courageously.

CHAPTER 3

CONQUER COURAGEOUSLY

DAILY STUDY GUIDE

DAY 1
Read Psalm 23:1-2

In what ways has God been a Shepherd in your life?

On a scale of 1 to *Oh-my-Gosh-I'm-Going-to-Starve-To-Death* how worried are you about material needs (a.k.a. food, money, and clothing)?

When we start thinking about things like financial aid and student loans, it's easy to worry about our future, but God isn't going to let us down. Make a list of the material needs you need to trust Him for.

What decisions are weighing on you right now? Are they a source of stress?

In Matthew 6 and Philippians 4 we are commanded not to worry. But that's a lot harder than it sounds. Below, pray over everything you just wrote down, handing it over to Him

Day 2
Read Psalm 23:3

We learned in the previous chapter what the Hebrew word for "restore" really means. What is it?

It's time to give our souls more than a tune-up. 1 John 1:9 tells us that "When we confess our sins, He is faithful and just to forgive us our sins and to cleanse us from all unrighteousness." Once we drop the weight holding us down, we are free to live. Think back over the last week. Is there anyone you need to forgive? Anything you need to repent of?

Have you ever made a decision based on what other people think of you? Explain.

Has God ever called you to do something that went against the opinions of others? What happened?

DAY 3
Read Psalm 23:4

Have you ever walked through the valley of the shadow of death? (I know it's not fun to remember these times, but it's so important to look back at the valleys God has brought us through.)

How did God bring you through that valley?

Describe a time when the Lord corrected you for something.

How did the Lord's correction feel?

All of us have different fears, but all of us fear evil. But He who is in us is greater than he who is in the world (1 John 4:4). I want you to think about the evil that you find most disturbing. I'm not going to ask you to list it here or talk about it with your study group, but I want you to remember that God has overcome everything evil in this world. Finish this sentence. "Jesus has overcome _____."

DAY 4
Read Psalm 23:5

Have you ever had an enemy?

If so, why were you enemies?

What is overwhelming you right now?

In the previous chapter we discussed the difference between bottling up our blessings and letting them run over into our lives. That requires letting of the areas in our lives we can't control. What do you need to let go of in order to let your cup run over?

Ephesians 6:12 tells us that "we do not wrestle against flesh and blood, but against principalities, against powers, against the rulers of the darkness of this age, against spiritual hosts of wickedness in the heavenly places." Whether we're fighting people or circumstances, they're not the real enemy. Our real enemy is simply trying to sidetrack us. Today, we're not going to let him win. Write a prayer for the people in your life that you would consider enemies. We are commanded by God to love them (Matt. 5:44). That doesn't mean we have to be best buddies with them or put our hearts in danger again. It means we need to forgive them and lift them up in prayer. As you pray, lift up the circumstances that stress you out. We won't ever be able to fight our real enemy if we're caught up in the people and circumstances of this temporary world.

Day 5
Read Psalm 23:6

In the previous chapter we talked about the definition of the Hebrew word for "follow." What is it, and what does it mean?

How long will goodness and mercy follow us?

Where are we going to dwell?

Let me tell you something, daughter of His. Your God desires to bless you! He didn't create us to live in stress and anxiety. His goodness and His mercy will chase you down all the days of your life. Your dare this week is to get up out of bed in the morning knowing that God desires to pour out blessing on you. Our God rose from the dead! Nothing can overcome Him. Compared to what Jesus faced on the cross, we have nothing to worry about. When worry claims us and we find ourselves becoming anxious again, we can come back to this list and find out what is making us fearful. Then we can deal with, repent of our fear, and move forward in goodness and mercy, dwelling in the house of our God forever and ever.

CHAPTER 4

ADORN VALIANTLY

"Many daughters have done well, but you excel them all."
Charm is deceitful and beauty is passing,
But a woman who fears the Lord, she shall be praised.

PROVERBS 31:29-30

Discovering Your Beauty

Christian Buzzwords

On my thirteenth birthday I got a present from a well-meaning older woman. It was a list of qualifications for godly young ladies. "DRESS MODESTLY!!!!!!" headlined the page like an ultimatum. The rest list was a slap in the face, even though a godly young woman was exactly what I wanted to be.

I grew up in a very legalistic community. My parents were careful to guard the grace of God in our home and not fall into the legalism that surrounded us. Even though it wasn't in my family, I was exposed to a lot of judgmental Christianity growing up, the kind of religion that give righteousness a bad name. Because of this, I've heard some very skewed definitions of words like virtuous, modest, and chaste. Even if we've heard those words a thousand times, we probably don't understand what they truly mean. If we did, we would be rushing after them. Instead, we tend to avoid them.

The enemy is deceiving us, which means we've got some debunking to do. And to do that, we'll have to go straight to the source. The original standard of virtue. The girl we all have a love/hate relationship with. I'm speaking of course of the Proverbs 31 woman.

Love Her, Hate Her, Imitate Her

In Proverbs 31 we are given a picture of a virtuous woman. It's an incredible passage brimming with household tips and parenting advice. Basically, it's the Pinterest of the Bible. However, it's been used as a baseball bat of authority to beat down Christian girls, which is heartbreaking. It was never intended to condemn us.

We've all heard verses from this chapter, even if we can't quote them off the top of our head.

> *Who can find a virtuous wife?*
> *For her worth is far above rubies.*

Proverbs 31:10

I've attended Christian conferences where this verse was taken completely out of context to prove that women should be slaves, never wear pants, and never leave the house. Then I discovered something. Want to see it? It's so cool! You'll never look at Proverbs 31 the same way once you know what modesty really means.

Chayil. It's a lovely little Hebrew word tucked into this verse. In my Bible it's translated "virtuous." But it ain't your Grandma's virtue. (Well…maybe it's your grandma's virtue. It depends on the grandma, I guess. Sorry. I'm getting off track.)

Chayil is a military word. It means "valiant, powerful, trained, and war-worthy." The word isn't just a depiction of a soldier, but an army, an unstoppable force. It also means "wealth" and "prosperity." All together it could be translated "a wealth of valor."

What do you picture when you think of virtue? It's probably not *chayil*. According to the Word of God, this girl's not just strong, she's Army Strong. What if that's virtue's true identity? What if it's not something we're supposed to look like, but someone we're supposed to be?

Proverbs 31 doesn't tell us what a godly woman looks like. Instead, it tells us what she does.

She trains at her craft (v. 13).

She works hard (v. 13).

She gets up early (vs. 15). Just to clarify. It says she gets up early, not that she wants to. There's hope for all of us.

She has a great mind for business (v. 16).

She's an athlete (v. 17).

She's confident in her talents (v. 18).

She prepares for her future (v. 21).

That's the kind of woman you and I are called to be.

A virtuous woman is the combination of beauty and strength. She's a warrior princess.

She's the kind of girl the right guy is looking for (v. 11) and the kind of mom every kid needs (v. 28). That's who virtue really is.

The "M" Word

At a certain river in Honduras the women were washing clothes. All of them were topless as they went about their work in the hot sun. A girl came running from the road shouting, "The men are coming!"

None of the women would dream of being caught so being immodest by the men of the village. So they dropped their work and hurried to cover...their legs.

Yes, their legs. In other parts of the world, it is completely natural for a woman to go topless, but she'd better not show off those sexy ankles.

Don't misunderstand me.

"Did she just say it's okay to go topless?"

No! Do not go tell your mother that's what you learned in Bible study this week. That's not what I'm saying. At all!

But there are those who would argue that modesty is simply a cultural hang up. But if it were, the Bible wouldn't mention it. So what does it really mean to be modest?

The Greek word for modest is *kosmios*. And no, it's not Greek for "ankle-length."

At its core, *kosmios* means that you don't draw attention to yourself.

Modesty is an attitude, not a dress code.

1 Timothy 2:9 says we should dress modestly, but for centuries people have argued over what "modest" means practically. It's the motivation behind our outfit. If we're dressing so people will notice us, it doesn't matter if we're dressing in a potato sack or a prom dress.

Take a moment to consider something. You have been given a holy responsibility. You have brothers in Christ who are human just like you. It's not fair to place all the responsibility for lust squarely on the guys' shoulders. I've heard Christians say that girls should dress however they want, and if the guys can't handle it, they need to deal with their filthy minds. That's just not fair. We all need to take our thoughts captive, but saying that lust is purely the guys' problem, is like saying that girls get pregnant all on their own. It's a two way street. There is responsibility on both sides. I don't want to get to Heaven and find out that my taste in clothes caused someone to fall into sin.

Another argument I've heard is "Don't we have freedom in Christ?" Yes! We do.

But beware lest this freedom of yours
Become a stumbling block to those who are weak.

I Corinthians 8:9

Modesty isn't a list of rules or a law of condemnation. It's our privilege to help our brothers in Christ. We have struggles of our own. Flaunting our bodies "because we can" is cruel to the men who are trying to keep their minds pure.

Modesty is also a gift. Because as much as we might hate to admit it, comparison is our weakness. We compare waist size, bra size, and hip size. But there is a confidence that comes with covering yourself. I feel more confident and more beautiful when I choose classy over sassy. There is a misconception that girls who dress modestly are ashamed of their bodies. Some people think that those who cover up have something to hide. That's not true. When I'm at the beach, I don't want to worry about who is or isn't looking at my butt. I want to enjoy the water and the sunshine without constantly sucking in my stomach. I want to be who God created me to be. I have full confidence that He has a special man chosen for me. This body is for his eyes only, not every guy who sees me in my swimsuit.

At the heart of Proverbs 31 we find this verse:

Strength and honor are her clothing;
She shall rejoice in time to come.

Proverbs 31:25

How many outfits in your closet could be defined by strength and honor? I love this verse because who doesn't want a wardrobe like that? Strength and honor are always vogue. A woman who dresses with confidence and dignity will win the respect of the men and women around her. She will be known for her personality, not her body. When I meet the man God has for me, I want him to know that his heart can safely trust me (v. 11), because I've been faithful to him before I ever met him (v. 12). Because dressing in the cheap way the world does, hurts *us* more than anyone else. There's a huge movement against men "objectifying" women, but the truth is, when we display our bodies for the world to see, we're objectifying ourselves. The enemy is lying to us, making us believe that our worth lies in our appearance. Every girl who has ever considered dressing modestly, has thought, *I'm not attractive enough to make anyone stumble.*

That is a lie from the pit of Hell. If you haven't listened to anything else in this chapter, listen to this:

You. Are. Darling!
The God who paints sunsets created you.
Don't you dare call His creation junk.

He created you to be a woman of strength and honor and valor. Don't buy into the garbage offered to you by this temporary world. Because when you are known for your strength and honor, you shall rejoice in time to come. You will laugh at the future. Your physical charms and beauties are going to fade, but a woman who fears the Lord will always be praised. God hasn't just called us to be pretty. He has called us to be war-worthy women who dress virtuously and adorn valiantly.

CHAPTER 4

ADORN VALIANTLY

DAILY STUDY GUIDE

Day 1
Read Proverbs 31:10-13

In the previous chapter we discussed a specific word from verse 10. Some translations render it "virtuous." In other Bibles it's called "worthy," "excellent," or "of noble character." What was the Hebrew word? And what does it mean?

What precious gem is a virtuous wife compared to?

This specific stone is interesting to study. They are not as strong as diamonds but far more valuable and extremely rare. In ancient times they used these gems to solidify the foundation of a building. They were durable, but nearly every ruby that has ever been mined is flawed. Isn't that a beautiful picture? We are meant to be tough, withstanding the pressure, and yet beautiful. We are meant to be precious yet not perfect. Search the Scriptures to find one other verse that talks about your worth and write it here.

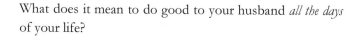

What does it mean to do good to your husband *all the days* of your life?

Are you a person who willingly works with her hands? If so, how? If not, what could you do to become one?

I think it's interesting that this is the first attribute of the Proverbs 31 woman. She works hard. Think through the areas of your life. Are there any areas where you're not giving it your best effort?

We're told in Galatians 5:9 not to grow weary while doing good. Below, pray for the areas where you are growing weary and losing strength. Because we're promised that in due season, we will reap if we do not lost heart.

DAY 2
Read Proverbs 31:25-26

How does this woman clothe herself?

When will she rejoice?

What two things come out of her mouth?

Three times in the book of Proverbs we're told that wisdom is more valuable than rubies. In the verses we studied yesterday we learned that a virtuous woman is also listed at the same priceless worth. This is no accident. Why is she so priceless? Verse 26 tells us. She is wise. How wise do you feel right about now? We want to be the kind of woman who opens her mouth with wisdom. Just to be clear, wisdom and knowledge are not the same thing. You can be a genius and still not be wise. None of us are anywhere close to the wisdom that is available to us in Jesus Christ, but don't worry. There's hope for us all. Look up James 1:5-8. What does it say about wisdom?

Okay. Now the dare. Go to your closet. Open the door. Look at your clothes. Look at them hard. We're told that a valiant warrior is clothed in strength and honor. Strength. Okay, there are lots of things that could exemplify strength, but honor, that's what sets her apart from the world. I want you to pray through your closet. I'm not going to give you a "modesty marker" and tell you what to wear. That is between you and God. But ask Him honestly if there is anything in your wardrobe that needs to change. Understand that He is by no means angry with you or ashamed of you, but if you and I want to live lives of freedom, we need to be willing to let go of the weights that hold us back. How did it go? (Be prepared to discuss this with your group.)

DAY 3
Read Colossians 3:12-14

What are we called in this passage? What two words describe us?

What five things does verse twelve tell us should be in our wardrobe?

❀

❀

❀

❀

❀

Which one of these is the hardest for you to put on? Why?

What are we to put on above all? According to verse 14, why?

What we wear as an attitude is so much more important than how we dress. However, when we understand who we are, everything else falls into perspective. We are the elect of God. He chose us. Why would we buy into the fashion game of the world? That isn't where our worth lies, and the more we buy into it, the easier it is to forget who we really are. When are you most likely to forget who you are in Christ?

Once we recognize the situations that weaken our sense of identity, we can deal with them. Below, write a prayer, asking God to help you remember who you are in Him and where you find your beauty.

DAY 4
Read Galatians 5:13-14

What have we been called to according to verse 13?

What warning does Paul give us?

What command fulfills the whole law?

Make a list below of everything Christ has set you free from.

Our freedom is such an incredible gift. Yet if we're not careful, we can use our freedom as an excuse and cause other people to stumble. Have you ever seen this happen among Christians? Without using names, describe what happened.

Our prescription for this problem is what Jesus called the second greatest commandment. (The first is loving God.) What do you think loving one another has to do with modesty?

DAY 5
Read Proverbs 31:29-31

What two things are deceitful and fleeting?

Who shall be praised?

What shall praise her and where?

Sometimes the choices we make for the Lord don't give us temporary pleasure. Sometimes they make the moment harder. It's hard to be the one that dresses modestly, that stays pure, that waits, but everything else is going to fade and pass away. The right choice is rarely the easy choice, but when we endure our own works will praise us. Pray for your endurance and perseverance as you chose to adorn yourself valiantly. Ask the Lord to continually show you what that means. When He does, obey Him, beloved. It will be worth it.

CHAPTER 5

RUN DAUNTLESSLY

Do you not know that those
Who run in a race all run,
But one receives the prize?
Run in such a way that you may obtain it.

1 CORINTHIANS 9:24

The Race of Faith

The Color Run

They call it the Happiest 5K on Earth.

Did I buy that? Not really. The pictures looked great online, but then, so do pictures of a Motel 6. I couldn't quite bring myself to believe that running three miles in the sweltering heat was nearly as fun as it looked. Then I got my bag of "racing swag" (a t-shirt, my racing number, a wrist band, and a rainbow headband) and was inclined to change my mind. Okay, so I'm easily bribed, but I was still somewhat cynical.

We left the house at 5:00 AM and drove an hour-and-a-half, meeting up with a group from our church. We, along with ten-thousand others, had come to experience The Color Run.

We were not disappointed.

In case you've never heard of The Color Run, you should know it's the coolest thing ever. Before you read on, Google it…just…just Google it. If you don't have Wi-

Fi at the moment, I shall do my best to describe to you the awesomeness of The Color Run with the futility of words. Because you and I have been called to a race of faith, and when you run in an actual race that picture takes on a whole new meaning.

The Good, the Bad, and the Sweaty

This morning I opened my Bible to Hebrews 12 and read the opening verse:

> *Therefore we also, since we are surrounded*
> *By so great a cloud of witnesses,*
> *Let us lay aside every weight,*
> *And the sin which so easily ensnares us,*
> *And let us run with endurance*
> *The race that is set before us.*

Hebrews 12:1

I used to read this verse and skip over it. I'm not particularly athletic, but I do run on occasion. This morning when I read it, I remembered The Color Run and got chills. In a few words the Color Run is…

Explosions of color.

Excitement like you've never seen.

Rainbows, tutus, and bubbles. (The tutus are optional, but life is short. Why not, right?)

The Color Run was even better than advertised. However, nothing can mask the fact of what it is: exercise. The motto of The Color Run is BE HEALTHY. BE HAPPY. BE YOU. They know that no matter how much color or glitter you coat it in, a 5K is a 5K. In my case, it was a 5K in 90 degree weather. Running in Kailua-Kona is no joke, even if it's just 3.2 miles. I wasn't exactly in the best of shape when I ran the race. There were plenty of times that I got side-cramps, felt sick, and had to stop for water.

Our race of faith is no joke. Granted, there's no other way I'd rather live life, but life gets hard. You know that. You're in high school. No matter how great your life is or how close your walk with God, you are going to have days that stink. Some days are so awful they are almost laughable.

I remember one day that was the epitome of bummer, Charlie Brown, death-by-a-million-paper-cut days. I was exhausted, but went to Youth Group anyway. Youth Group did not go well that night. I was deeply upset about something but trying not to show it. After the Bible study we went to play a game outside. BLAM! The basketball hit my face so hard that my tear ducts opened and started draining. Enter the mocking of my peers. "Oh my gosh. Are you seriously crying?" *No. I'm not crying. I'm trying really, really hard not to throat-punch you right now.* (I didn't say that to him. I thought it…with my inside voice.) After a long drive home, I poured out my woes to my parents, including miserable situation at Youth Group and the following fate of my face. "I think I'm just really tired. I'm going to bed." I then proceeded to trip and fall down the stairs. I remember laying in a crumpled heap at the bottom of the stairs, hearing my mom's frantic worries from above me. "I'M (hiccup) FINE!" I yelled up at her between sobs.

Yeah. That was a horrible day.

Even if our life is amazing, all of us have those days when life hits us like a basketball to the face. But here's the promise of Hebrews: We're not alone.

Hebrews 11 is known as "The Hall of Faith." It tells the stories of Old Testament heroes who walked by faith. The stories of Noah, Abraham, Sarah, Enoch, and Rahab are all recounted in this passage. The writer was so passionate that he had to hold himself back.

...for the time would fail me to tell of Gideon and Barak
And Samson and Jephthah, also of David and Samuel
And the prophets:
Who through faith subdued kingdoms,
Worked righteousness, obtained promises,
Stopped the mouths of lions, quenched the violence of fire,
Escaped the edge of the sword, out of weakness were made strong,
Became valiant in battle, turned to flight the armies of aliens.

Hebrews 11:32-34
(And all the sci-fi fans said, "Amen!")

The heroes mentioned in Hebrews 11 didn't just have bad days. They had mockings, scourgings, chains, and imprisonment. They were stoned, sawn in two, tempted, slain with sword, afflicted, and tormented (vv. 36-37). These guys were the real deal. They didn't just get a little sweaty. They got a little bloody. They gave their lives for the service of the Kingdom, and that's where Hebrews 12 starts. *Therefore since we are surrounded by so great a cloud of witnesses...*

Every time you see a "therefore" in the Bible you need to ask yourself what it's there for. It's a transitional word that means "with all these things in mind," or "because of everything we just talked about..."

We are being cheered on by a "cloud of witnesses."

Do you realize that the heroes of the faith are cheering you on?

On your rough days, when you go through trials, when you face temptations, those who have gone before us are like the spectators at the finish line, excited to see us finish our race of faith. I don't know about you, but I want to make them proud.

Bonus!

As my friends and I raced through the heat, we came upon "Color Stations" where volunteers stood by to bombard us with a cloud of magical color dust. (It's really dyed corn starch, but "magic dust" sounds so much better.) This is what sets The Color Run apart from every other 5K. You can run a 5K whenever you want. You don't even need to wait for someone to organize the thing. Just lace up those running shoes and go for it. You could even try to recreate the color run. I'm sure your neighbors won't look twice at you throwing handfuls of cornstarch out in front of yourself while you're jogging. But it's not the same.

When you share the Lord with people, many of them will question, "Why do I need God?" There are plenty of "successful" people in the world who don't believe that there is a God. All you need to do is take a look at their life. What they have is a sad imitation of what God has for us. Eastern meditation might be relaxing, but it ain't got nothin' on spirit-filled prayer. Temporary happiness might be nice, but compared to the joy Jesus has for us, it's a handful of dust.

People love to fling a particular question at Christians. "What if you're wrong? What if there is no God, and when we die there's nothing?"

Answer: We've missed nothing.

Even if you were to take grace and salvation out of the picture, living for Christ is still the best life out there.

There is no other religion that offers and delivers on the promise of a peace that can't be shaken and a joy that can conquer any crisis.

We get to stand in light no one else could imagine and face the darkness with a courage no one else could understand. These are the bonuses of the Run of Faith. These are the explosions of light and color that we cannot experience outside of Christ.

The Finish Line

Of course, the best part of any race is the finish line. In The Color Run the home stretch is a barrage of bubbles. After you cross the finish line, you are handed a water bottle, a granola bar, and a package of magic color dust. Our group finished the race and wandered around with our color packets wondering what they were for.

One of the volunteers finally explained, "Oh, that's for the after party."

The Color Run after party was one of the best things I've ever experienced. Seriously. It's up there with

Disneyland and Star Wars. In a crowd of thousands, you dance, you party, and realize your mom knows all the words to *That's What Makes You Beautiful* because she's singing them at the top of her lungs. ("You know this song?")

Then there is a moment. It's a moment that The Color Run is famous for. It's a moment that has won photo contests and been captured by countless Go Pros. The DJ on stage tells you to open your package of magic dust. Then he starts a countdown.

5-4-3-2-1!

At the same moment everyone releases the pack of color they've been given, tossing it up in the air. The crowd is enveloped in a cloud of color that can be seen for miles.

Our Run of Faith is an amazing way to live, but the best part is the after party. Heaven is going to be the best after party ever, which makes everything else worth it.

> *For I consider that the sufferings at this present time*
> *Are not worthy to be compared*
> *To the glory that shall be revealed in us.*

Romans 8:18

What is glory? It's almost impossible to define. We know that glory hovers around God. It's His beauty. It's His holiness. We've all heard about God's glory. But according to this verse and others like it, that same glory dwells in us. 2 Corinthians 4:7 says that "we have this treasure in earthen vessels." From everything we read about glory in the Scriptures, it's like a glow stick. We have it within us, but we don't really know what it is. When

Christ returns for all of us, these earthly vessels crack, and every heart that's ever believed in Jesus glows to life. All of us have been given a portion of God's glory, like that packet of magic dust. To someone who doesn't understand, it might look like cornstarch in a plastic baggie.

But we know better.

At the perfect moment, God is going to count down. That glory He has hidden inside of us will be released as we meet our Savior in the air. We will be enveloped in the clouds to be with Him, dwelling in that glory forever. Then the sorrows, the sufferings, the difficulties, the bad days will seem so small that they won't be worth comparing.

So don't give up, beloved. Run hard. Run dauntlessly.

CHAPTER 5

RUN DAUNTLESSLY

DAILY STUDY GUIDE

DAY 1
Read 1 Corinthians 9:24-27

What two sports are described in this passage?

What's our goal in the Race of Faith?

How are we to run and fight, according to verse 26?

What is required to remain in the race?

In your mind, what is the hardest part of the Race of Faith?

How can we run with certainty? How do we know that the prize we're striving for is real?

What this verse is prescribing is a spiritual work out. In my garage there is a sheet of paper pinned to the wall that lays out what a good work out looks like, different exercises that bring different muscle groups into submission. If you were to make a work out sheet for your faith, what would be on it? We don't want to be legalistic (20 min. of prayer. 30 min. of Bible reading), but it's good for us to think of new areas to stretch our faith so that we get a well-rounded "work-out." Your dare this week is to create a list of different things you can do to spiritually challenge yourself and do as many of them as you can. Be ready to share how it went with your group.

DAY 2
Read Hebrews 11:30-35

What allowed all the miracles listed here to occur?

How many stories are mentioned here? Are there any you don't recognize?

Most of us are probably familiar with David, Samuel, and Samson. Pick one other hero of faith listed here and study them, writing what you find out about their faith.

- ❀ Rahab: Joshua 2
- ❀ Gideon: Judges 6
- ❀ Barak: Judges 4
- ❀ Jephthah: Judges 11

Of all the accomplishments listed in Hebrews 11:33-35, which three do you find the most impressive and why?

Your God is able to do all this and more. Write down a specific time in your life when you saw faith result in miraculous circumstances, and be prepared to discuss it with your group.

DAY 3
Read Hebrews 12:1

Who are these witnesses? (Hint: We discussed it in the previous chapter.)

What are we to lay aside?

What are we commanded to do?

If you had to pinpoint where you are on your Race of Faith, where would you be? The starting line? The water break? The heat of the race? Where would you say you are? Why?

We are called to lay aside two things: every weight and the sin which so easily ensnares us. They're not the same thing. We've talked a lot about confessing our sin and seeking the Lord's forgiveness, but sometimes what is holding us back isn't sin. Maybe it's another area of our life that we need to let go of. It could be anything from food to entertainment to a relationship that's unhealthy. Below, write a prayer asking God to show you what is weighing you down.

DAY 4
Read Hebrews 12:2

What are we to look at as we run our Race of Faith?

Why did Jesus endure the cross?

Where is He now?

My brother is a competitive swimmer. One of the things he has to do to improve his technique is watch the pros. How long do they glide before taking a stroke? How do they make that flip-turn when they hit the wall? That's how we're supposed run our race, watching Jesus, the Author and Finisher of our faith. That's one of my favorite titles for Jesus. He wrote the rules of the race, but He also finished it. It's hard to take orders from someone who's never experienced what you go through, but Jesus has been through all of it. He endured more than any of us ever will. He endured the cross for the joy set before Him. And that joy was you. What struggles are you experiencing in your race right now? How can Jesus' example help you in your specific circumstances?

DAY 5
Read 2 Corinthians 4:16-18

What is dying and what is new every day?

How long is our affliction in light of eternity?

What is this affliction gaining us?

What is temporary, and what lasts forever?

As we run our race, we need to keep the finish line in mind. This run of ours is wonderful, but it's not the goal. Heaven and God's glory are our goal, our prize. We can't be disheartened when we fall, when we struggle, and when we suffer. It's just a moment compared to what God has in store for us at the finish line. But if we look at our circumstances, we'll only be discouraged. Which is why we can't look at the visible, tangible things around us. We have to keep our eyes on the prize that's going to last forever. What visible areas of your life distract you from the eternal things?

Now my fellow runner, I'd like to pray for you. You're not alone in this Race of Faith. We're all running together, side by side, and we're going to finish strong if we don't lose heart.

Lord, I lift up this sweet daughter of Yours. I know You see how hard she is working and how much she wants to please You. I pray that You would give her an extra burst of energy today and that You would open her eyes to see the spiritual battle being waged around her. Lord, show her the weights she needs to drop and the sin that's going to ensnare her if she's not careful. God, I pray that You would be that sip of ice-cold Living Water that she needs to get through one more mile of this race. Help her not to grow weary. Strengthen her and cheer her on, and Lord show her what a powerful athlete she truly is.

In Jesus Name,
Amen.

CHAPTER 6

FIGHT RELENTLESSLY

For though we walk in the flesh
We do not war according to the flesh.
For the weapons of our warfare are not carnal
But might in God for pulling down strongholds,
Casting down arguments and every high thing
That exalts itself against the knowledge of God,
Bringing every thought into captivity
To the obedience of Christ.

2 CORINTHIANS 10:3-5

Spiritual Warfare

The Mondays...and the Tuesdays

Monday started out so well. I had my cup of coffee in my Tinkerbell coffee mug, my chair pulled up to my desk, my laptop open and awaiting my pearls of wisdom. *Who's going to write this Bible study? I'm going to write this Bible study. Oh yeah. I got this.*

Fast forward about four hours. I was curled up in a ball sobbing. *What makes me think I can write a Bible study?! Why do I even try? I'm going to fail. Why waste my time?*

Tuesday wasn't much better.

Wednesday I didn't even make it past 10:00 AM before the doubt came out of left-field and flattened me. The voice of doubt wouldn't stop as I tried to keep typing and forge on through my blubbering.

Who do you think you are? Do you really think anyone is going to listen to you? I mean, have you looked in the mirror lately?

It was then that I finally recognized that voice for what it was and realized what was going on.

I was in a battle, had been in a battle since Monday, and I needed to start acting like it.

I opened my Bible to Ephesians 6 and started reading. As I did, everything started to clear.

For we do not wrestle against flesh and blood,
But against principalities, again powers,
Against the ruler of the darkness of the age,
Against spiritual hosts of wickedness
In the heavenly places.

Ephesians 6:12

You and I are in the midst of an invisible battle, and while it might feel like a case of the Mondays...or the Tuesdays...or the Wednesdays, we need to wake up and realize that we don't have to walk defeated. We've been called to win this thing.

I don't know about you, but I find it really hard to fight in a battle that I can't see. But God has given us all the weapons and the tools we need to be victorious (Eph.1:3). So let's not waste one more day.

Take Off the Mask

The box-office-breaking *Star Wars: The Force Awakens* was my favorite movie of 2015. It was worth every bit of the hype, and while I could go on about all of the things that made it a fantastic work of cinematography, there was one part that stood out to me more than any other.

The villain of the movie, Kylo Ren, is a Jedi on the dark side. Throughout the movie he wears a mask as he goes about killing innocents and wreaking havoc. He's a bad dude, but half-way through the movie something interesting happens.

The heroine dares him to take off his mask. As he reaches to take it off, you are preparing yourself for the face of evil to be revealed from beneath that mask, but when you see his face everything changes.

You suddenly realize that the villain these heroes are worried about is nothing more than a whiny, arrogant brat with anger-management issues. This is shocking (and somewhat disappointing for those of us who were expecting a roguishly handsome bad guy). But it changes the game for the heroine. Because it's in that moment that she realizes she can beat him.

In the same way, we need to unmask our enemy and realize where we stand in this war. Very often, we get the wrong idea about our enemy. We think he is some equal and opposite force to God. Not so.

In Isaiah 14 we're told the story of how our enemy came to be. He was a created angel that rebelled against God and fell from Heaven, taking a third of the angels with him.

In other words, he's a whiny, arrogant brat with anger-management issues.

He hates God, but can do nothing to hurt Him, so he goes after God's children. Namely, us.

And while that might sound frightening, we need to remember that Satan was beaten when Jesus rose from the dead. He's already lost. We're already on the winning side. The devil knows his days are numbered and that in the end he is going to lose. He's not trying to win, he's just trying to drag down as many humans as he can along the way.

Before we get any farther, you need to know something. Satan cannot touch your soul.

> **If you have accepted Jesus Christ, you are covered in the Blood of the Lamb, and you will never lose your salvation.**

The devil knows this, and isn't going to waste his time going after something he can't have. When he tries to mess with us as Christians, he's not trying to condemn us to Hell. He's trying to shut us up. He knows that after the Blood of Christ, the most powerful weapon we have is our story of faith, and he doesn't want us to tell it. But today he's not going to win.

Sleight of Hand

Have you ever been in a card game with someone who tipped their hand? They turned or dropped their cards, and you instantly saw what they were holding. That can happen on a spiritual level too.

I remember the first time the enemy tipped his hand with me. I was seventeen.

As a senior in high school, I was desperately trying to figure out what to do with my life and paralyzed by my fear of failure. What if I launched out into this world and fell flat on my face? What if I was a disappointment to the people who'd invested in me, or worse, what if I broke their hearts? What if I couldn't take the pressure?

Day after day I lived in this fog of fear and doubt.

In 2 Corinthians 12:7, Paul talks about a season of spiritual warfare in his own life when the enemy "buffeted" him. That word buffet might sound like a medieval fencing tactic, but the actual definition is "to continually punch in the face."

Have you ever felt that? Like the enemy has got you in a corner and is drilling you over and over? That's how I felt for a decent portion of my senior year.

Then everything changed.

I watched at a distance as a kid raised in a Christian home, whom I had known my whole life, walked away from the Lord. Throughout high school he had rebelled against the faith his parents had taught him, and he lost hope. One morning my family got the call that he had taken his own life.

I was devastated, but as my grief began to clear over time, another emotion started to burn inside me. I was angry.

Not at this kid.

Not at the situation.

Not at God.

I was angry at the devil.

I remember the day it clicked, the day the devil tipped his hand. I realized that all of the fear and the doubt I had been walking in was part of a strategy. Satan was trying to shut me up and render me useless. All of a sudden I felt like I was standing toe-to-toe with the devil himself, looking my enemy in the eye, seeing him unmasked for what he truly was. I remember the freedom and the strength that rushed through me as I said the words out loud.

"I am sick and tired of what you do to teens, and your tricks aren't going to work on me anymore. There are people out there dying in the darkness, and here I am in the light, afraid I might make a mistake. You can try all you want, but you will never shut my mouth."

Suddenly, the Lord started bringing people to my mind, young people who were wide open to the lies of the enemy. For the first time, I got it. I understood the reason why the enemy was trying to shut me up.

It was you.

He never wanted me to get out, to tell my story, to expose him for the fraud that he is.

Right then and there I made a promise.

"I'm going to tell them. I am going to tell them what a liar you are. You are not going after these kids, not on my watch. Jesus Christ has already defeated you, and I'm on His side. So, you know what? Back off. And Shut. Your. Mouth."

That day I started seeing victory in my life. It was a battle. There were days that I fought every moment against the voice of the enemy. I've been fighting that same voice all week, but you know what? My God is still winning.

Taking Action

You and I are the ones in the light. We need to see the enemy for what he is and expose him. Because you need to understand that he hates your guts.

Satan can't have your soul,
but he would settle for your mouth.

He knows what a powerful force you are. You are his worst nightmare, and that is why he is after you, after your witness, after your prayer life, and after your family.

He loves to sidetrack us and make us think that the problem is physical. But the problem isn't your parents. The problem isn't your siblings. It's not that one kid at school or that teacher you can't stand. Your problem is that you have a very real enemy who wants you to go down in flames.

One of my favorite movie moments is when the heroine realizes the threat. The action music kicks in and there's a montage of training where she learns to defend herself against her enemy.

You and I need to suit up and learn how to fight back. We need get into the Word and find out what it says about our battle and our victory. We're not going to win this thing by accident. We need to be intentional. We need to pull out our spiritual weapons. We have been given an entire suit of spiritual armor, and so many of us don't even know how to use it.

We need to be on our knees before the Lord, because you can talk a good game to the devil all you want, but the truth is, without the Lord we will fall into the enemy's traps over and over. We need to find our strength in the Lord and let Him bring us the victory.

Cue the music.

Start the montage.

You and I need to learn how to wage an invisible war, how to take a punch and get back up. If you and I are going to be warriors for the kingdom, we need to learn how to take a stand against the hosts of wickedness. We can't afford to be afraid of our enemy. Wherever you are today, whatever the enemy is throwing at you, don't give in. Get up, sister. Take your stand. Fight relentlessly.

CHAPTER 6

FIGHT RELENTLESSLY

DAILY STUDY GUIDE

Day 1
Read 2 Corinthians 10:3-4

How does Paul describe the weapons we've been given?

What are these weapons good for?

In ancient times a stronghold was a fort or a place of defense. It's where the army ran when they were losing. When we're losing our battles in life, we run to a physical stronghold instead of running to the Lord. That might be an old habit or an addiction. And when I say addiction, I'm not just talking about drugs and alcohol. We can be addicted to things that seem harmless, but they distract us from running to the Lord. We can be addicted to food, people, or entertainment. When the enemy comes after me, I want nothing more than to curl up in my bed with my chocolate and my Netflix. That's not a sin, but it's no way to win a war either. Think through your own life and write down the things that you usually run to instead of running to the Lord.

You can be a black belt in several disciplines of martial arts. In the same way, we can learn different spiritual ways to discipline ourselves. This week, I dare you to learn a new spiritual discipline. Below are three different spiritual defenses. Pick one, and practice it every day this week.

- Scripture Memorization: Start memorizing one chapter of Scripture. (Yes, the whole thing.) You don't have to get it all in one week, and it doesn't have to be a long chapter. Pick a Psalm or a chapter that you really love. Read it everyday, write it out, say it to yourself, or put it to music until you have it committed to memory. If you're not sure what to memorize, I would suggest Psalm 121, John 15, or Ephesians 6.

- War-like Prayer: All of us know that prayer is important, but few of us really understand the power of prayer. Pick one spiritual struggle your life and pray like you've never prayed every day this week. Don't just fold your hands and close your eyes. Get specific. Include details. Write down names. Search up Scriptures that apply, write them down, and hang them on your wall. Don't relent in praying for this area of your life until you start seeing victory.

- Serious Worship: Spend time every day this week in worship. Find some good worship music, and really enter into the presence of the Lord. Praise Him for Who He is. If you're a musician, learn new worship songs to sing, or maybe even write some. Either way, learn what it means to come before the throne and worship your God.

Day 2
Read 2 Corinthians 10:5

To give this some context, go back and read verses three and four again to remember what we're talking about. What four categories are our weapons good for?

*

*

*

*

Yesterday we talked about tearing down the strongholds in our lives. The next thing our armor is good for is casting down arguments or imaginations. This doesn't mean any old argument. This is specifically talking about arguments against our faith, the times we doubt. Share about a time when you struggled with doubt. We all have them. And the best way to deal with doubt is by pulling it out into the light and exposing it for what it is.

The word for "thoughts" in verse 5 is the Greek word *noema*. It's the same word used in 2 Corinthians 2:11 when it says, "Lest Satan take advantage of us, for we are not ignorant of his devices." That word "devices" is the same word for "thoughts." In other words, these aren't just every day thoughts. These are thoughts and whispers and doubts planted in our minds by the enemy. Now the enemy can't take over mind or force us to do things. That's not how it works, but he *can* tell us lies and remind us of our weaknesses and failures. Go get a separate sheet of paper. On this sheet of paper, write out every lie the enemy has ever told you. Now rip that paper to shreds. Below, write the truth of who God says you are.

The battle begins in us. Before we can go fight for our brothers and sisters on the front lines, we need to examine our own lives, tear down our strongholds, cast down our doubts, and take our thoughts captive before they have time to fester and throw us off our game. We can't live our lives believing the lies that the enemy throws at us. Today practice taking your thoughts captive and forcing your mind to submit to Jesus. Keep your eyes on Him no matter what. Maybe that means writing Scripture on your hand so you remember. Maybe that means telling a friend to keep you accountable. Do whatever it takes to take back control of your mind and turn the tide of this battle.

Day 3
Read Ephesians 6:12-15

What *don't* we fight against?

What four things are we fighting against?

❀

❀

❀

❀

Why are we told to put on the whole armor of God in verse 13?

What pieces of armor are listed in this passage?

❀

❀

❀

❀

❀

❀

When it says we don't wrestle against flesh and blood that means that our fight isn't against anything we can see. All of us are fighting something. It could be circumstances or people or anything else that keeps us down and discouraged. What "flesh and blood" things are you most tempted to fight against?

Two times, back-to-back, we are told to stand. So often, we think we're supposed to storm ahead, but the victory is God's job, and sometimes there are days when all we are able to do is stand. Describe a time when you had to stand firm for the Lord against the enemy.

Back in Day 2, we wrote down a list of who God says we are. Go back, and look at what you wrote. That is your belt of truth. That's the piece of armor that holds everything else together, who we are in Christ. We also confessed and repented for our strongholds in Day 1. That's the breastplate of righteousness. When we confess and repent of our sins, God sees us as righteous. Satan would love for us to feel guilty and ashamed. That's why it is so important to confess our sins immediately to our Father in Heaven. The next piece of armor is the preparation of the gospel of peace. In Day 2 we talked about taking our thoughts captive. That is the key to peace of mind, not letting our thoughts rule us but ruling our thoughts and forcing them to submit to Jesus. But putting on our armor isn't a one-time thing. We have to do it on the daily. Before you go out into your day, remind yourself of who you are in Christ. Confess to your Lord, and take your worries and your doubts captive.

DAY 4
Read Ephesians 6:16-18

What quenches the enemy's fiery darts?

Most of the armor is there for our protection, but there is one piece that is meant to do some damage to the enemy. What is it?

What does Paul command us to do in verse 18?

The armor listed here is important. These are the big guns, the epitome of our defense system. Our faith shields us when everything seems hopeless. Our salvation protects us from the most fatal of wounds. The Word of God attacks our enemy. If I were to ask you how good you are with your Sword, what would you say? Do you think you could hold your own in a spiritual battle?

Here's a little Sword practice for you. These are three real questions that Christians get asked all the time. In your Bible there are verses that answer these questions. Pick one and find the Scripture that answers the question.

❀ How do you know the Bible is true?

❀ If God loves us, why do bad things happen?

❀ How is Christianity different from any other religion?

DAY 5
Read Romans 8:31-39

What did God give us, according to this passage?

In verses 38 and 39 Paul makes a list of things that cannot separate us from the love of Jesus Christ. Which one is the hardest for you to believe? Why?

What does this passage say we are?

Believing that we are the conquerors is the first step to our victorious life. No matter what you are facing, Jesus has already overcome. We're already on the winning team. It's time to act like it. What is an area of your life that you need the Lord to conquer? Write it below, praying for His deliverance. Then, dear one, believe Him for it. Trust Him to take care of it. Every time you doubt, give it to Him again, and trust Him to conquer on your behalf. Then live in your freedom, because you, darling girl, are more than a conqueror!

CHAPTER 7

TRANSFORM ENDLESSLY

Therefore, if anyone is in Christ,
He is a new creation;
Old things have passed away;
Behold, all things have become new.

2 CORINTHIANS 5:17

Saying Goodbye to the Old You

The Ghost of Puberty Past

Have you ever seen an old picture of yourself and wanted to gag? I have. Yesterday in fact. A friend texted me a picture from several years ago. My pubescent self grinned relentlessly back at me. The conversation that followed had me laughing for the rest of the day.

Me: That picture right there is EXACTLY why I wrote a book for middle schoolers. We all need help.

Her: Hey, but it all turned out pretty great. Puberty hit ya like a bus, and now you're drop dead gorgeous.

Ah, yes. A bus indeed. Words fitly spoken.

No matter how old we are, none of us like to be reminded of our past selves, the old us. We all give a little shudder. We remember the things that everybody else forgets. It's like our most humiliating moments are burned forever in our memories. It's one of the more horrendous parts of growing up. We hate remembering the braces, the drama, and the crash-course in hormones.

Then we "grow up" and move on, but every now and then there is that certain someone or that one circumstance that drags the old you out of hiding. For the most part, I consider myself a very different person than I was at the age of thirteen. But when I'm around certain people I'm amazed at what comes flying out of my mouth.

I don't like to remember my old self, but believe it or not, we're not supposed to. Now I don't mean the outward appearance. Adults keep assuring me that I'll look back with fondness on my middle school days…maybe…someday. But I'm talking about the "me" that was a little more selfish and a little less patient. It should make me shudder. The Bible calls that old version of us our flesh. It might sound like a deep concept, but who better to explain deep theological concepts than Disney Pixar?

Inside Out

Inside Out is one of my favorite movies. I cried…twice. (Bing-Bong and I were bros, okay? This movie was very emotional for people—like writers—who make a living off of imaginary friends.) If you haven't seen the movie, it all takes place inside the head of a twelve-year-old girl named Riley. Inside Riley's head there are five "emotion" characters that determine how she thinks and reacts to any given situation. Joy, Sadness, Disgust, Anger, and Fear work together as a team to help Riley react to life.

Surprisingly, the movie parallels a very spiritual concept. Only in the spiritual world it's not our emotions that determine our life. The Bible names three characters inside of us that determine who we are and what we want in life. Imagine these three as the characters running the control panel.

The first character is your mind. Your mind is obviously what you use to think and make decisions. However, your mind is very easily influenced. While we might think that our mind is what makes the decisions in our lives, the truth is that the mind does whatever it's told by the other two characters at the helm.

The second character is our flesh. Our flesh is everything selfish and sinful about us. Every time we reach for the biggest cookie, tell a white lie, or make a selfish decision, it's because our flesh felt like calling the shots. Before we know the Lord, the flesh runs our life. The flesh has a lot of names in the Bible. It's also called our "sin nature" or "the old man." It's the human side of us that causes us to sin. While it would be nice to blame all of our sin on the devil, it's our flesh that causes us to be tempted in the first place. It's what caused Eve to eat the fruit in the garden and Judas Iscariot to sell Jesus for thirty pieces of silver. It's our desire to get ahead and get what we want. Before we're saved, our flesh runs the show, bullying and bossing our mind into doing whatever it wants.

The third character is our spirit. Okay, stick with me here. Everyone on earth has a spirit. It's the little eternal sparkle that sets us apart from animals. It's the part of us that knows we're meant for something more. Before we're saved, that spirit inside of us is dead. Decisions in your head are made thusly:

The flesh whines and complains and screams for what it wants.

The spirit—being dead—says nothing.

The mind is then bullied into doing whatever the flesh wants.

But then, BAM! Jesus shows up, the Holy Spirit enters us, and our spirit comes to life. Our flesh can never have the same power it did before. Suddenly the Holy Spirit is running the show, telling our mind the decisions we should make.

Salvation paralyzes the flesh, but it's not dead.
Our flesh still has a mouth.
A loud mouth.

And it still whines and complains and screams for what it wants. Our mind is then torn between what our flesh wants and what Jesus tells us is right. From that moment it's a battle.

For the flesh lusts against the Spirit,
And the Spirit against the flesh;
And these are contrary to one another,
So that you do not do the things that you wish.

Galatians 5:17

The Old Man

When I was in my high school girls' study, we learned about this concept for the first time. We had to study

Romans 6 in our homework, which talks about putting our flesh or our "old man" to death. A friend of mine didn't understand the concept and came back the next week wide-eyed, asking, "Who the heck is this old man? And why on earth are we supposed to kill him?"

Our "old man" is simply the old us. The part of us that used to be ruled by the flesh. Now you might not have a lurid past of sin and regret, but all of us have had moments we're not proud of.

Have you ever made the easy choice instead of the right choice? That's the war described in Galatians 5.

All of us have given into the flesh. We give into it more than we know.

A year ago I thought I had my flesh under control, but the Bible's clear. It's not something that just goes away. We're not supposed to put up with it. We're at war with it. If we don't take it seriously, the flesh is going to start manifesting in ugly, self-centered ways. We've already talked about the devil, our very real enemy, but so often, the things we struggle with aren't even his doing. We're at war with ourselves just like we're at war with him.

In Chapter 1 we talked about the life of peace and joy Jesus wants us to live. As long as the flesh is allowed to rule in our lives, we won't be able to truly enter into our rest. Because the flesh always wants more. It's constantly making us think about ourselves. *Am I happy? Do I have everything I want? Do I feel safe? What if I don't get what I want? What if I have to settle for less than I deserve?*

We've grown up in a culture that tells us being happy and feeding our flesh should be the goal of our life.

When we don't get what we want, our flesh throws a tantrum. And we let it, eventually giving it exactly what it wants over and over again.

Most of you have probably heard the story of the black dog and white dog, but what you might not know is that it is *not* an ancient Cherokee Proverb. This lovely little metaphor was first told by none other than the beloved Reverend Billy Graham.

The story tells of two dogs, a black one and a white one. The two dogs are constantly locked in a battle. Which dog wins the fight? Whichever one you feed.

When we form the habit of following our flesh, it will only get stronger and control us even more.

When we obey the Holy Spirit, we are strengthening those muscles of submission that will determine who we truly are when we have to make a split-second decision.

A Lovely Eulogy

A few years ago I attended a women's event where we were challenged to write a farewell speech to our flesh. When someone dies, people love to give speeches. Since we're supposed to put our sinful habits to death, we wrote eulogies to our sin natures.

It might sound like a strange way to look at things, but Jesus was clear that we are meant to be radical about our sin. In the Sermon on the Mount Jesus told us that if our right hand causes us to sin, it's better to cut it off and throw it away rather than let it lead us into temptation

(Matt. 5:30). Did He really want us to cut off our limbs? No. Scripture clearly tells not to punish ourselves the way the world does. What this verse, and others like it, are saying is that we have to stop babying our sin nature. That might mean cutting off a friendship or a habit or a form of entertainment that is damaging to us and our walk with the Lord. It might mean walking away from something or someone we love in order to follow Jesus. And yes, it's going to hurt. And no, the world won't understand. But we were never supposed to be like them anyway.

And be not conformed to this world,
But be transformed by the renewing of your mind,
That you may prove what is that good
And acceptable and perfect will of God.

Romans 12:2

We are meant to constantly be renewing our mind. Just like fighting our spiritual battles, defeating our flesh isn't a one-time thing. It's a decision we make day-by-day and even moment-by-moment. We won't be complete until we reach Heaven, but no matter how many times we mess up, Jesus isn't going to give up on us. He Who began a good work in us will complete until the day of Christ (Phil. 1:6). Don't settle for a stagnant life. Transform endlessly.

Upon the Death of Me
In disgusted memory of the me that used to be.

The acclaimed child prodigy, the star of every show
The center of attention, don't deny it, 'cause I know.
How your heart burned for glory, how your only goal was fame.
And when you left this sallow earth, they all would know your name.

You were a brilliant actress. You knew how to play the part.
You had everyone believing in your humble, contrite heart.
Had your parents done athletics, you would have excelled to your
shame.
But as it happened they served Jesus. So you learned to play that
game.

There was just one problem in your crafty, clever plan.
Because one day I encountered the perfect Son of Man.
For the first time I could question, just who it was that ran my life.
And I found you there on the throne, the queen of all my strife.

The mistress of perfection, the cruel princess of pride.
I saw the monster that you were, and that was the day you died.
I'd had enough of all your games, You were dead now, I was sure,
And I thank my God every day that I saw you for what you were.

The murderer of many, the leading cause of spiritual SIDS,
The terror of the Christian Mom, The plague of pastor's kids,
The showy, shiny, dazzler, the faith-killer no one suspects,
I still shudder when I think about how I could have been next.

Your funeral was very short, held one night in my room.
No one else attended because no one misses you.
I was plunged beneath God's perfect grace, and watched your ashes
float away.
It was not a gaudy drama. You would have wanted it that way.

You died some years ago now, and I get along just fine.
So relieved that my desires are no longer mine.
God is on the throne now, the place where you once sat.
You're dead. But you know something? I haven't treated you like
that.

Your pictures are still on my walls, 8x10s of Glossy Greed.
I'm still surrounded by the comforts that you told me I need.
Is this your music on my iPod? Are those your books on my shelf?
And when I hate the ones who've wronged me, this room fills with
your smell.

It's time for a remodel. All your stuff is coming down.
I don't want to act for one more day, like you are still around.
Because when Jesus rescued me He made sure my life would show it.
With Him, I've joined the winning team. You've lost. And we both
know it.

CHAPTER 7

TRANSFORM ENDLESSLY

DAILY STUDY GUIDE

DAY 1
Read Romans 12:1-2

How are we called to present ourselves?

What does verse 2 command us to do and why?

The word for "beseech" is the Greek word *parakleo* which means "to encourage, exhort, or comfort." But it's not the squishy, pillowy comfort we think of. It's a form of encouragement from a teacher to a student or more specifically, from a coach to an athlete. In essence, the word *parakleo* means "to dare." Paul is daring us to sacrifice our wants for the Lord. This week's dare: Say no to your flesh. Give up one thing. Just for the week. It could be anything—TV, sweets, social media. So often, the problem with our flesh is that we think we don't have a problem. The most successful time I've ever had at conquering my flesh was when I committed to exercise. It wasn't an issue of body image. I wasn't trying to lose weight, but every time I put on my running shoes, my flesh was practically screaming, "I don't wanna go!" And I finally got to a place where I could laugh and say, "I don't care what you want. We're going." Either give something up, or take on something hard this week, and don't make a big deal about it. We're told in Matthew 6:17-18 that we're not supposed to fast for other people to see but for God. However, it's important that we have accountability. Be prepared to record and share with your study group how your challenge went this week.

DAY 2
Read 2 Corinthians 5:17

What are we in Christ?

According to this verse, what does that change?

What differences do you see in the lives of people who don't have Jesus and people who do?

What transformations have you seen in your own life? (If you, like me, said a prayer when you were three and can't remember your life before Christ, simply record how the Lord has transformed you since you got saved.)

Below, write your own eulogy to your sin nature. You can reference the one I wrote in the previous chapter. Don't worry. It doesn't have to be a poem. It doesn't even have to be long. You're basically writing a "break-up letter" to the person you used to be, telling them goodbye for good. Be prepared to share it with your group.

Day 3
Read Galatians 5:16-18

What one command sums up the entire concept of the taming your flesh?

Why don't we do what we wish?

The battle against our flesh is simple. The key to conquering it is simple. The reason we get discouraged is because we get "simple" confused with "easy." Simple isn't the opposite of hard. Simple is the opposite of complicated. Dead-lifting two-hundred-and-fifty pounds is simple. It doesn't require mathematic equations. But it's not anywhere close to easy. It takes training. It takes practice. It's hard. Conquering our flesh is the same principle. It's hard, but it's simple. Paul tells us the answer right here: Walk in the Spirit, and you will not fulfill the lusts of the flesh. What does it mean to walk in the Spirit?

What does the enemy tempt you with? Maybe it's fear or cynicism. Maybe it's popularity and the opinions of others. All of us are different, but it's important to know our own weak points. Psalm 91:3 says that the enemy is like a hunter setting a snare for us. A trap has to have bait. Below, make a list of areas you are most tempted to give into your flesh?

Look again at the list you just made. Now give it to the Lord in a prayer below. We're told in the Lord's Prayer to ask Him not to lead us into temptation, but to deliver us from evil (Matt. 6:13). He has promised that He will never lead us into more temptation than we can stand (1 Cor. 10:13). He wants us to overcome, but that takes perseverance on our part. Ask Him for endurance as you start the battle against your flesh.

Day 4
Read Galatians 5:19-26

How many works of the flesh are listed here? How many fruits of the Spirit?

What do you think is the worst sin listed in the works of the flesh? Which one is the smallest sin?

Paul doesn't list them as big sins and small sins. They're all just sin. Some may cause more damage than others, but sin is sin. "Selfish ambition" is listed in the same verse as "witchcraft." But here is what I love about this verse: It's simple. We live in a world that is so politically correct that we can no longer discern what is right and wrong. While we are never supposed to put ourselves in God's place and judge people (Matt. 7:1), we are told to use discernment. Jesus said that we would know people by the fruit we see in their lives (Matt. 7:20). This isn't about knowing what's in the hearts of others. We need to know what's in our own heart. Which fruit of the Spirit are you working to perfect right now? And what has the Lord shown you?

We have been redeemed. When we accepted Christ's death on the cross, our flesh was crucified. It can't control us anymore, but it can still tempt us. Jesus poured out His blood so we could live in the spirit, yet so often we choose to walk in our flesh instead. Below, make a practical plan for the situations ahead of you today. Write down the different things that might tempt you to walk in the flesh.

Based on the list you wrote above, come up with ideas on how to walk in the Spirit in those specific situations. Be prepare to share how it went with your study group.

DAY 5
Read Philippians 1:6

What does this verse promise us?

Why does this encourage you?

What "good work" is this verse talking about?

The word for "confident" here describes a process. It means to be persuaded until you believe, then to stand confidently in what you believe. How can we be confident that the Lord is continually changing us?

How has the Lord changed you from the person you used to be?

What do you want Him to change next?

Be confident, sister. He is not going to give up on you. The work He is doing is so magnificent, but we have to let Him work. One of my favorite quotes from C.S. Lewis talks about this in his book *Mere Christianity*.

"Imagine yourself as a living house. God comes in to rebuild that house. At first, perhaps, you can understand what He is doing. He is getting the drains right and stopping the leaks in the roof and so on; you knew that those jobs needed doing and so you are not surprised. But presently, He starts knocking the house about in a way that hurts abominably and does not seem to make any sense. What on earth is He up to? The explanation is that He is building quite a different house from the one you thought of - throwing out a new wing here, putting on an extra floor there, running up towers, making courtyards. You thought you were being made into a decent little cottage: but He is building a palace. He intends to come and live in it Himself."

Do not fear, dear one. He is making you into something beautiful.

CHAPTER 8

GO BOLDLY

But you shall receive power
When the Holy Spirit comes upon you;
And you shall be witnesses to Me.
In Jerusalem, in all Judea, in Samaria,
And to the ends of the earth.

ACTS 1:8

Sharing Your Faith

The Best Job Ever

It was my first time leading a girl's retreat. I was sitting on the back porch, looking out at the stunning view of the valley. It had been a lovely, memorable time, and it was drawing to a close.

But the Lord wasn't finished with me that weekend.

I heard the screen door slide open and turned to see one of the girls. I invited her to join me, and she sat down across from me, tears brimming in her blue eyes.

I asked her what was wrong.

She was shaking as she said, "I don't know if I'm saved. I don't think I'm a Christian. I want to be sure I'm going to Heaven."

It was my turn to get teary-eyed. It was the dream-premise, the moment every Christian hopes for.

After talking with her a few minutes, we prayed together, and I watched the Holy Spirit flood into her life. I had never seen salvation like that. It was like a light turned on behind her eyes, and she could see everything for the first time.

And that was when I knew.

I was hooked.

This was all I wanted to do for the rest of my life. I had watched as a soul walked into the light for the very first time. There is no feeling like it.

That was the day I caught the ministry. And as you can see, I caught it bad. This thing ain't ever going away.

So often, when we talk about witnessing to our others, we feel guilty, but evangelism was never meant to be a feast for the guilt-monster. It's our calling, our adventure, and our joy.

Proper Plant Care

Orchids only bloom one month out of every year. Last May someone gave me a little potted orchid, and to my amazement, it lives! (I tend to have a rather black thumb when it comes to plants, especially delicate ones.)

I have kept it alive all this time, watering it and setting it in the afternoon sunlight on my desk. I recently realized that since I'll be traveling this summer, I won't be here to see it bloom. In fact, the person who planted the orchid probably never got to witness the fragile pink flowers that it produces only in the merry month of May.

And that is how salvation works.

We want it to be instant. But I'll bet that the person who planted that orchid didn't go through an identity crisis when it didn't bloom right away. *Oh no. I'm doing something wrong. What am I doing wrong?! I planted it three hours ago and it isn't doing anything. Lord, why?!*

Likewise, I don't expect the plant to sprout blossoms every time I water it. It's an orchid not a Chia Pet. It takes patience and time.

But isn't that how we expect our witnessing to be? *I've talked to them about the Lord three times, and they're not saved yet. I must be doing something wrong!*

Or God put you in their life to plant the seeds of salvation.

Or He's using you to water the seeds someone else planted.

Even if we never see the blossoms, even if we don't know the outcome until Heaven, it's God's job to bring the increase. And He's good at His job. He's been working on this whole redemption thing for a while now.

One of the biggest lies about sharing our faith is that if people aren't getting saved, we're doing something wrong.

That's not necessarily true.

Statistically, a person needs to hear about something at least six times before they'll even consider trying it.

This applies to witnessing too. In the case of the girl I prayed with, she had gone to Sunday school as a little girl and had many Christian friends. There were prayer warriors who had been praying for her salvation for years. She already had a great foundation and knew what she was getting herself into. I just got to be the lucky bystander that got to pray with her.

But that's not always the case.

Sometimes we don't get to be the one to see people saved. Sometimes we're the one that has to pray for years. But the enemy would love to convince us that we're failing in our Christian walk if we're not calling thousands of people to repentance.

For a long time I thought I was a terrible Christian because I hated street witnessing. I'm an outgoing person. I like people. But sharing my faith with total strangers gives me the willies. There. I said it.

But the Lord showed me that street witnessing just isn't my gift. Get me a guitar, lock me in a room with a bunch of kids, leave me there for a few weeks, and I'll be fine. But don't send me into the streets with tracts to pass out. I will probably return crying in about twenty minutes.

So often we wish we had the gifts that other people had. We'd love to be a great evangelist like Billy Graham. Who knows? Maybe you are. Maybe that *is* your gift. But not all of us were designed to have the same gifting.

And He Himself gave some to be apostles,
Some prophets, some evangelists,
And some pastors and teachers,
For the equipping of the saints
For the working of the ministry,
For the edifying of the body of Christ.

Ephesians 4:11-12

If we all had the same gifts, the church would be one big blob of identical people. Instead, the church is teeming with diversity and difference, yet it's still one body with one goal: Tell this broken world that Jesus came to save them.

Perhaps the most famous evangelist in the Bible—other than Jesus Himself—was the Apostle Paul. His job description was to travel from town to town, preaching the gospel and leading people to Jesus.

And yet even he didn't always get the joy of bringing people into the Kingdom. In his letter to the Corinthians Paul spoke about himself and another missionary of his day.

I planted, Apollos watered,
But God gave the increase.
So then neither he who plants is anything,
Nor he who waters,
But God who brings the increase.

1 Corinthians 3:6-7

To You, With Love

What's your favorite time of year? Mine is Christmas! Hands down. Not even a question. For the entire month of December I am Buddy the Elf. Some people find that Christmas dulls as you get older.

As I've gotten older Christmas has only gotten more magical for me, but I have an advantage. I love presents. A friend of mine told me that she hates it when people spend money on her. She asked me if I'm ever disappointed by what's in the shiny package.

Nope. Not ever. And that's coming from someone who got a coconut for Christmas one year (long story). I should add that I live in Hawaii. Coconuts are nothing special. They are the pinecones of the tropics. Moving on.

I guess I just never got over the whole concept of presents. The idea of someone thinking of you, getting something (even if it's a coconut), and wrapping it in shiny paper still makes me smile. After that, nothing is disappointing.

Matthew 7:11 tells us that God loves to give good gifts to His children. That doesn't just mean the blessings in our lives.

Like we see in Ephesians 4:11, we all have different gifts as God's children. Often, Christian young people freak out when they don't know what they've been called to do. I was one of them. I spent a lot of time in high school freaking out because I didn't know what my spiritual gifts were.

But that's the definition of a gift. You're not supposed to know what it is. It's a surprise locked away inside you. God loves to surprise His kids. When the time is right, God will reveal it to us. Our Savior has given us everything we need for life and godliness (2 Pet. 1:3). We already have the tools. We just need to know how to use them.

I'm not the type of person that leads people to Christ in the grocery store. I've found that my most effective way to witness is to simply be there. When I meet someone who doesn't know the Lord, I don't start preaching to them. I simply try to live out my faith every single day. I'm not always the one that gets to lead them to the Lord, but I might get to be "that one Christian girl" that was always there for them, that didn't judge them but stood on the truth and reflected Jesus Christ.

Sometimes we feel that our gifts aren't important enough, that they aren't big enough, but that's not true.

We get to play a part in the glorious story of redemption. That is no small task.

We are called by God to charge into the darkness, to storm the gates of Hell, and stand against the power of this world.

Then He said to them, "The harvest is truly great,
But the laborers are few;
Therefore pray the Lord of the Harvest
Will send laborers into His harvest.

Luke 10:2

That's you and me. We're the laborers. Sometimes we're called to plant, and sometimes we're called to water, and sometimes we get to see salvation spring up and thrive. I promise you, that there is nothing like it. So wherever you are, whatever God has called you to do, don't grow weary.

Find your gift.

Head into this dark world.

Wherever you have been called to go, sister, go boldly.

CHAPTER 8

GO BOLDLY

DAILY STUDY GUIDE

DAY 1
Read Acts 26:12-18

Who is speaking in this passage?

What story is he telling?

A testimony is the story of how we came to know Jesus. It's one of our most effective tools when we're witnessing to nonbelievers. In this passage Paul is sharing his testimony with Herod Agrippa (a ruler in Israel). There are many different kind of testimonies. Paul had an incredible one. Jesus literally came to him in a blinding light. What kind of testimony do you have? Were you saved as a little kid, or did the Lord get a hold of your heart more recently?

I got saved when I was three. I don't remember it at all. Many of you were probably raised in the church, but that doesn't mean you don't have a testimony. The fact that you are still walking with Him is a powerful testimony to His glory. Even if you don't remember getting saved, our testimony comes when we realize how real or how big our God is. Imagine that you are sharing with an unsaved friend and they ask you, "Why do you believe in God?" They're not asking for scientific evidence or a theological explanation. They want to hear your story. What would you tell them? (Be ready to share this with your group.)

Day 2
Read Acts 1:4-8

What is happening in this scene?

What question did the disciples ask Jesus?

What was His response?

When would they receive power?

Where would they go?

Has God ever called you to witness to someone outside of your comfort zone? What happened?

Below, make a list of your unsaved friends, and spend a few minutes praying for each one of them. Pray that God will reveal Himself to them. Pray for them, their family, and their school or job. Whoever this friend is, they are walking in darkness, and the only One who can reach them is the Lord. He might use you to do it, but you'll never lose by lifting them up in prayer.

Day 3
Read Ephesians 4:11-14

What five gifts are listed here?

*

*

*

*

*

Why are they important, according to verse 12?

What is this passage protecting us from, according to verse 14?

The idea of spiritual gifts is one of the biggest arguments in the church at large. Sadly, the discussion of spiritual gifts has done exactly what Paul warned us it would. So many people have taken this concept and twisted it. It's easy to be tossed to and fro by every wind of teaching. The Bible is very clear. There *are* spiritual gifts. That's what this passage is all about. God has given each of us a gift to be used for His glory. However, that's not an excuse to take our spiritual gift and start beating people over the head with it. First of all, our spiritual gift probably has a lot to do with our personality. Circle the statement below that sounds the most like you.

❀ I love to work behind the scenes where no one can see me.

❀ I love to meet new people and find it easy to talk to strangers (except the creepy ones).

❀ I love explaining things clearly to others and seeing their eyes light up because I helped them.

❀ I love being able to give up my time or money to help someone in need.

All of us have different personalities and that affects our spiritual gifts. For years, I wondered what my spiritual gift was. Then I realized that my favorite thing in the world was to take a section of Scripture, dig into it, and explain to those around me. Bible teaching isn't something I was forced into. It's something I love. If God let you pick anything. If He told you that you could go anywhere and do anything for His glory, what would you do?

DAY 4
Read 1 Corinthians 3:6-11

What two pictures does Paul give for witnessing?

According to verse 7, how important are we to this process?

Just to be clear, none of us fall into only one category, but if you had to pick, which one do you think you do the most?

- ✿ Planting (Being the first person to ever tell someone about Jesus)

- ✿ Watering (Sharing with people who have heard but aren't sure what to believe)

- ✿ Harvesting (Bringing people to the Lord)

- ✿ Tending (Ministering to people who are already saved)

You dare this week is to search out your spiritual gift. Spend time in prayer, asking God to reveal your spiritual gift to you. Don't be discouraged. Whatever God has called you to do, He has also equipped you to do, and it's so important to the Kingdom. When you've prayed wait on the Lord to see what He shows you. If you still aren't sure what your spiritual gift is, ask a spiritual mentor who knows you. This could be your parents, your youth leader, or your pastor. Write what you discover about your spiritual gift below.

DAY 5
Read Luke 10:2-3

What does the Lord need more of?

What picture does He give the disciples as He sends them out?

There are people all over the world, waiting to hear the gospel, wondering where God is. Is there an area of the world you feel particularly drawn to? Maybe it's Africa. Maybe it's your own backyard. Wherever your passion is, pray over that area today. Pray specifically for the people in that area, and pray that the Lord would send laborers there to share the gospel. Write your prayer below.

Jesus' next command to His disciples is to spread the gospel. Not all of us have the freedom or the calling to leave our home, but we don't have to go anywhere in order to be laborers in the harvest. Where is God calling you to go today? How can you be a laborer in His field right where you're at?

CHAPTER 9

WALK CONFIDENTLY

Do not fret because of evildoers,
Nor be envious of the workers of iniquity.
For they shall soon be cut down like the grass,
And wither as the green herb.
Trust in the Lord, and do good;
Dwell in the land, and feed on His faithfulness.

PSALM 37:1-3

Blocking Out the Haters

Haters Through History

It is not the critic who counts; not the man who points out how the strong man stumbles, or where the doer of deeds could have done them better. The credit belongs to the man who is actually in the arena, whose face is marred by dust and sweat and blood; who strives valiantly; who errs, who comes short again and again, because there is no effort without error and shortcoming...who at the best knows in the end the triumph of high achievement, and who at the worst, if he fails, at least fails while daring greatly, so that his place shall never be with those cold and timid souls who neither know victory nor defeat.

Theodore Roosevelt
April 23, 1910

That is one of my favorite speeches of all time, because haters are nothing new. We've all got 'em, and they're not going anywhere. So we'd better learn how to deal with them.

One of my favorite stories in history is about a man named Sir Oliver Cromwell. He had overthrown the monarchy and become the Lord Protectorate over England. He and his men were walking through the streets as the crowds cheered them on. One of his men commented that he was glad to see that they had the nation on their side. Cromwell replied, "Do not trust to that. For these very persons would shout just as much if you and I were going to be hanged."

I always remember that quote when I receive feedback of any kind, whether it's a compliment or a criticism. People are fickle by nature. When you succeed, they will praise you. When you fail, they'll say they told you so. That's why popularity is so short-lived.

We are always going to face criticism, especially if we choose to live for Christ, and believe it or not, that's good news.

"You have enemies? Good.
That means you've stood up for
something sometime in your life."
-Winston Churchill

As young people, we are going to face naysayers every time we try to do something worthwhile. And we're not the first ones. Psalm 37 has a lot to say about those who make fun of God's people. It was a Psalm written by David near the end of his life. If anyone knew about haters, it was David. When he was a teen he killed a giant. We all know that story, but what we forget is what brought

David to the battlefield. The road was lined with naysayers. Three specific groups stand out in the story, and surprisingly, they are the same three kinds of haters we face today.

The Bros

As you may recall, David was the youngest of eight. He had seven older brothers, and to say that he was picked on doesn't even come close. He wasn't just the youngest kid. He was the youngest kid that everybody forgot about. When the country's prophet invited the family to a sacrifice, David was left home like Cinderella from the ball. But the prophet Samuel soon saw that God hadn't chosen any of Jesse's older sons. Then faster than you can say bippity-boppity-boo, he found the scrawny runt of the family and anointed him as the next king of Israel.

I'm sure that went over well with the fam. Nothing like having a man of God look at you and say, "Sorry. Not you. Do you have—I don't know—a brother?"

Ouch. It probably earned David plenty of dirty looks from his older brothers.

We know that they weren't David's groupies, because a few chapters later when David shows up on the battlefield, his brother's response is priceless.

"Why did you come down here?
And with whom have you left those few sheep in the wilderness?
I know your pride and the insolence of your heart,
For you have come down to see the battle."

1 Samuel 17:28

As an older sibling, I find this hilarious. I can hear Eliab, his anger "aroused," taking all of his frustration out on his kid-brother. "What are you doing here? Don't you have stupid sheep to watch? Don't give me that look. You think you're so awesome. You just *had* to come see the battle. Is that it?"

And David said, "What have I done now?"

1 Samuel 17:29

Being the kind of teen that doesn't buy into the garbage this world offers is going to draw attention to you.

Our peers are the first group of haters we'll come up against. They will come at us with the same attacks whenever we try to step out.

1. Why?

This question doesn't seem like it should throw us, but it does.

Why aim for the best grades when you could just pass?
Why say no when everyone else is doing it?
Why?

If we're going to deal with the haters, we need to know our "Why." We need to have conviction in the things we do and the choices we make. We need to have an answer for the hope that is within us (1 Peter 3:15). People want to know why you believe the things you do, even if they're not haters. We need to be sure of what we know. Do we just believe this stuff because our parents told us to or because it was our decision? Why did we choose the Christian walk?

2. That's irresponsible.

There are always things that stand between us and our destiny. Normal, real-life things. And the naysayers will always be there to remind you of how big your problems are.

You think God's calling you to that college. "What about the money?"

You think God wants you on the mission field. "What about ISIS? What about Ebola?"

You think God's calling you to step away from an unhealthy group of friends. "What about being a good witness?"

Haters are great at shooting excuses at us. If we try, we can come up with a hundred excuses that sound practical and even spiritual, but that's all they are—excuses.

If God is calling us to something, He's most likely calling us away from something else, and we need to be willing to let go.

Let me clarify: That's not an excuse to be irresponsible. I'm not saying that the next time your mom tells you to do the dishes you should tell her that you're not feeling called. Yeah. That won't go over well. But haters have the sickening talent of reminding us of the normal things, the safe things. They make faith sound irresponsible and naïve.

3. I know you.

Haters love to point out our weaknesses. In the case of David, his older brother reminded him that he was prideful and insolent and simply wanted to be in the middle of the action. Eliab's words have a superior tone of, "Step aside, helpless citizen. Leave it to the professionals."

The critics and scoffers love this move. Jesus himself was a Prophet without honor in his own town (Matt. 13:57). The people who saw Him work miracles in Nazareth said, "Is this not the carpenter's son?" (Matt. 13:55)

Last summer I went to the graduation party of a friend I hadn't known very long. Throughout the evening I noticed I was relaxed and able to enjoy myself because there was no one there I'd grown up with. Don't get me wrong, those are some of my deepest friendships, but there was a certain relief to knowing that the people at my table had no memories of my terrible awkward phases or my stupid mistakes. Sometimes, our closest friends can also be our biggest critics because all they have to do is say, "I know you." Now hopefully, we have healthy, godly friendships. But sometimes the people who know us best love to pull the "I know you" card to discourage us. Our best defense against this is knowing who we are in Christ, because He still desires to use us, no matter what our peers say.

The Grown-Ups

The next critic David faced was King Saul, who told him that there was no way David was going up against a giant.

For you are a youth, and he a man of war since his youth.

1 Samuel 17:33

Saul was honestly trying to help. He was a more experienced adult, lending some advice to a hot-headed kid with crazy life goals. All of us have adults in our life who want us to succeed, but don't want to see us get hurt. Just to be clear, I'm not talking about the authority God has placed in your life. I am so thankful that the Lord gives us people whether it's our parents, pastor, or youth pastor to let us know when our decisions are unwise. Those people are to us what the prophet Samuel was to David, but most of us have a few King Sauls in our life too. I'm talking about adults who motivate through fear and horror stories. We've all met them.

"Want to go on the mission field, do ya? Did you hear about that one missionary who was gored to death by a rhinoceros?"

Yeah. Them. You know them. They are honestly trying to help, but instead of guiding through wisdom and common sense, they guide through criticism and fear. Then they pile opinions on you.

1 Samuel 17 gives us the perfect picture. Saul reluctantly agreed to David's plan on one condition: Saul wanted David to borrow his armor. But when David put it on, it was heavy and got in his way. He told Saul, "I cannot walk with these," (v. 39).

> When we try to please others, even if they are adults whom we respect, we will find ourselves weighted down and unable to walk in what God has called us to do.

When adults criticize our decisions we tend to have one of two responses. Either we give into their spirit of fear, or we get defensive. Neither response is the right one. I love David's response to Saul. He doesn't give into Saul's doom and gloom, but neither does he start defending himself and bragging. He simply tells the king what God has already done in his life.

Your servant has killed both lion and bear;
And this uncircumcised Philistine will be like one of them,
Seeing he has defied the armies of the living God.

1 Samuel 17:36

When God is calling us to step out in faith, we need to have our lion and bear stories ready for the haters. We need to remember what God has already delivered us from and stand on it. We don't have anything to prove. Because it's not us that's doing the work. It's the Lord.

The Giants

And lastly, the final critic David had to face was the giant himself. For us, that's the devil. Our enemy is known as "the accuser of our brethren" (Rev. 12:10). Satan is the hater that messes with us the most because his voice is the loudest of them all without making a sound. Unlike our earthly critics, the enemy—just like Goliath of Gath—isn't simply jealous or trying to be helpful. He is out to grind us into the dust and destroy our walk of faith. He's not playing games, but we have been given the strength and weaponry we need to take him out.

> *Therefore, submit to God.*
> *Resist the devil*
> *And he will flee from you.*

James 4:7

Here's the thing about David: His critics were right about him. He *did* want to see the battle like his brothers. He *was* too young to fight Goliath. He *should have* worn the king's armor. According to every statistic and professional, he should have lost that battle. The critics were all right about David.

What stings most about the naysayers, is that they are right about us. They might know us, but they don't know our God.

Praise God! It's not about whether or not we're qualified. They might know our failings, but they don't know what God can do through them. They haven't seen the way He delivered us from our lions and our bears.

They can criticize all they want, but when we face our giants, when we take our steps of faith, "all the earth will know that there is a God in Israel" and in each of us. You know what? The haters might be right about us, whatever we want to do for the Lord might fall through completely. But I, for one, would rather fail while daring greatly for Jesus Christ than be counted with the cold and timid souls who know neither victory nor defeat. The Lord is on your side, beloved. Walk confidently.

CHAPTER 9

WALK CONFIDENTLY

DAILY STUDY GUIDE

DAY 1
Read Psalm 37:1-3

Who are we told not to fret about? Why shouldn't we fret about them?

What four things are we to do instead?

*

*

*

*

Below make a list of people that make you fret.

Often, the enemies in our lives cause us to fret because we fear they'll get ahead of us, or that they won't get what they deserve. But the Lord's promise to us here is that He sees they're deeds and it's not our job to worry about them. Every time I'm worried about one of the naysayers in my life, it's because I'm not finding my contentment in Him. Of all five commands listed in verses 3 and 4, which one do you find the hardest to obey?

Lift this area of your life up to Him. The Lord wants to teach you how to trust Him and delight yourself in Him. Ask Him to show you practical ideas on how to obey the command you listed above. Write your findings below.

DAY 2
Read 1 Samuel 17: 20-27
(If you're not familiar with the story, check out the first twenty verses of the chapter.)

Where was David headed and why?

What was Israel's response to Goliath of Gath?

What was David's response?

Have you ever seen something taking place in today's culture that you knew was wrong, but nothing was being done about it? Explain.

The things you just listed are the "giants" in our culture. Everyone else is afraid of them. Everyone else has given up. Sometimes it takes the moxie of a teen to stand for what is right. What cultural issues or generational "giants" would you like to take down in your lifetime? How could you do it?

Lift these giants up to the Lord. He sees them, and He has given you a passion for these issues for a reason. Maybe these are the battles you're meant to fight in your lifetime. Ask the Lord to show you how you can practically take a stand against the giants in our culture.

DAY 3
Read 1 Samuel 17:28-30

Who was the first hater David faced?

What did he have to say to David?

When was the last time you were criticized by your peers?

What was your response?

Have you forgiven them?

Often, when our friends or siblings criticize us, it cuts deep. Even if we don't like to admit it, we care about their opinion. But if we're getting our identity from our friends, we are eventually going to be crushed by their criticism. Instead, be the kind of person that encourages other people's dreams. We all have people in our lives who are younger than us and look up to us. Think of someone you can encourage this week, someone younger than you who has a crazy dream. As much as we hate the dream-killers in our lives, it's all too easy to turn right around and be one. Make an effort to encourage them this week, and be prepared to share how it went with your study group.

Day 4
Read 1 Samuel 17:31-39

What did Saul think of David's bright idea and how did David respond?

When was the last time someone told you that you were too young to do something and how did you respond?

Growing up, I loved the Disney Channel show Phineas and Ferb. Maybe it's because I'm the nosy older sister with two younger brothers. Maybe it's because I can relate to two little kids who love to do crazy things like climbing up the Eiffel Tower, discovering something that doesn't exist, or giving a monkey a shower. (The throw-back is free.) My favorite part of this adorable cartoon was that sometimes in their escapades, these two ambitious brothers would get cornered by an adult who would ask, "Aren't you kids a little young to be building a roller coaster?" Every time their response was the same. "Why yes. Yes, we are." David's response to Saul is almost identical. "Aren't you a little young to be a giant-killer?" "Why yes. Yes I am." So often we get defensive of our youth, but it's nothing to be ashamed of. When adults corner us, we don't have to defend ourselves. Because it's not about us. It's about what God is doing through us. But in order to have that confidence, we need to have our lion and bear stories. How have you seen God prove His power through you?

Day 5
Read 1 Samuel 17:40-51

What was Goliath's only goal?

What David's response?

This is the classic example of Biblical trash talk! Regardless of what God has called to do, we all face the same giant: the devil. His only goal is destroy us. How has Satan lied to you?

Once again, we need to take note of David's response. He didn't get tripped up on physical weapons. When Goliath started trash talking, David didn't respond by saying, "Oh yeah? Well I've got a pretty sweet sling-shot." No. He said, "But I come to you in the name of the Lord of Hosts." We have that same weapon. When the devil comes at us with his taunts and his lies, our best response is the Name of Jesus. Right here is where faith comes in, because David's response isn't timid. It isn't in a mousy whisper. Sometimes we need to stand toe-to-toe with our enemy with some holy trash-talk of our own. David didn't tell his giant, "Well maybe…someday…you'll get what you deserve." He said, "The Lord *will* deliver you into my hand…on *this day*…" (v. 46 emphasis mine). We need to enter our spiritual battles with that kind of confidence. Now there were years of fighting between the Israelites and Philistines after this, but that day was the day that everything changed. That was the turning point. We are going to be in a battle as long as we walk on this earth, but today can be the turning point. Today can be the day that we face our enemy down and say, "The Lord *will* deliver you into my hand, and everyone will see that God is at work in my life." Don't hesitate, sister. Today is the day. I dare you to take a stand on the victorious ground your Savior won for you. Write your response to the devil's trash talk below.

CHAPTER 10

DARE GREATLY

"For I know the thoughts that I think toward you,"
Says the Lord, "thoughts of peace
And not of evil, to give you a future and a hope.
Then you will call upon Me and go and pray to Me
And I will listen to you.
And you will seek Me and find Me,
When you search for Me with all your heart."

JEREMIAH 29:11-13

Finding God's Will for Your Life

Blue's Clues, **College Counselor**

How can I find God's will?

The first time I asked this question I was sitting on my living room floor watching *Blue's Clues*. From the ten-inch TV screen, Steve of the green-striped shirt and the Thinking Chair was informing me that I could do anything that I wa-anna doooooo. I remember wondering if Steve had ever heard of Divine intervention.

Then and there I decided that I needed to find my life goal. By age four I had it figured out. I proudly announced to my parents that I was going to be a missionary veterinarian. (Hey. It might be a thing. Someone had to take care of the pets of those in the foreign field. Why shouldn't it be me?)

I was politely assured by one and all that I didn't have to have my whole life figured out. After all, I was only four.

Then I woke up in my senior year of high school. The only headway I'd made in the career department was giving up on my theological veterinary goals.

Okay, so maybe you didn't want to pet puppies for Jesus, but when we were young, Sesame Street made growing up sound so easy. It's not until we're older that it starts to set in. We need to have goals if we're going to look like a sane adult.

I spent much of my senior year face-down, begging the Lord for direction. In fact, all my friends did. Every week we would get together for Bible study and take prayer requests. Every week our requests were the same: "I still need to figure out what I'm doing with my life. So…yeah…"

In high school the world expects you to have your life figured out ASAP. As you near your senior year, it seems like every person you've ever known corners you with that ever-irritating question: So what are your plans?

If I had a dime for every time I got that question it would have paid for four years at Stanford.

But as Christian young people, we want more than just the "smart" decision for our life. We want God's will for our life. It's what we all want to know. We're terrified of getting it wrong. What if we fail? What if we miss His will?

Fear not.

In my senior year, I discovered a passage of Scripture that gave me some peace of mind. I studied it, memorized it, and hung it on my bedroom wall. There were days when Deuteronomy 30 was all that got me through the day.

For this commandment which I command you today
Is not too mysterious for you, nor is it far off…
…but the Word is very near you, in your mouth
And in your heart that you may do it.

Deuteronomy 30:11, 14

I think that most of the time "finding God's will" is a lot less complicated than we make it. God wants to reveal His will to us. The Scriptures promise that if we seek Him, we will find Him, when we search for Him with our whole heart (Jer. 29:13).

Practical Steps

The best way we can find God's will for our life is by knowing our God. We need to be studying His word and spending time in prayer, letting Him speak to us, and learning to discern His voice from our own doubts and desires. We're promised in Psalm 37:4 that if we delight ourselves in the Lord, He will give us the desire of our heart. This is the first and most important step in finding God's will.

> If we know Who God is, it's a lot easier to know what He wants for our lives.

The second step is to ask godly authority in our lives. If our parents are our spiritual leaders, we should be making time to talk and pray with them about our futures. If not, we need to be able to talk to our Pastor or Youth

Leader. We don't have to make these decisions alone. That's why the Lord gave us our brothers and sisters in Christ. It's our responsibility to reach out and find them, because the Lord is faithful to put them in our lives.

When we've completed steps one and two, sometimes we still don't have clear direction. I know I didn't. There is no verse in the Bible that says, "Thou shalt go to such-and-such college and prosper there."

I wish. No such luck.

I remember the day I realized what God was calling me to do. It came out of nowhere. It surprised me and threw me for a loop, but then it made so much sense.

When we're planning our lives we like to give God choice A or B.

Should I go here or there?

The thing is, God loves to choose C.

But that wasn't one of the choices!!!

God won't be put in a box by us.

So often, we limit ourselves because we are limiting our God.

In my senior year I gave God two options:

A. Bible College
B. Regular College.

And guess what He chose.

C. Stay.

Stay? *Stay* here? Stay *here?* Lord, I don't think you understand. I've got goals. There are things I want to do. I can't just *stay*.

But He wasn't calling me to stay and do nothing. After I graduated I went into the ministry. I started writing and publishing my books.

I can't tell you how much joy and contentment I've found in His will. I made the decision to follow Him, even if that meant taking the road less traveled. Even if it meant abandoning the plan I'd had my entire life. Even if it meant explaining why I wasn't going to college for the one-thousand-four-hundred-and-eighty-second time. Even if it meant bearing people's disappointment in me. And believe me, I disappointed people. People I respected told me that I would never get saved if I didn't go to college. Some pulled my younger brothers aside and said they hoped that they wouldn't follow my bad example. I had to let go of my people-pleasing and care about God's call more than other people's comments.

I found my calling when I stopped trying to fit God's plan into my choices and started fitting my choices in God's plan.

Now what He's calling you to do is probably completely different from what He called me to do. I have a friend who graduated the same year as I did. We used to call each other and bawl over the phone about how we were never going to figure our lives out. The same time I realized that I was supposed to stay and work on my writing, God called her to a college thousands of miles away. Both of us have grown so much in the Lord since then. God isn't restrained by one plan or another. He has something unique and individual for every one of us.

What if I Miss It?

It's the million-dollar question. What if we miss God's plan for us? What if we're too distracted? What if we're not spiritual enough? What if we can't discern His voice from the devil's? What if we go down the wrong path by accident?

But that is what is so beautiful about Deuteronomy 30. The Lord's will isn't up in Heaven. It's not across the ocean. God's will is in our heart and in our mouth that we may hear it and do it. Honey, you're not going to miss it.

Our God can find us wherever we are.

Moses was sheep-sitting when the burning bush appeared (Ex. 3:1-2).

Elisha was plowing a field when the local prophet called him into the ministry (1 Kings 19:19).

Peter and John were fishing when Jesus said, "Follow Me," (Matt. 4:18-19).

Nothing exciting. Nothing important. However, that doesn't mean they were doing nothing. They weren't sitting on the couch, pounding Doritos, waiting for God's will drop out of the sky.

They were simply doing what they'd been doing every day as long as they could remember. They were working their nine-to-five jobs. They weren't freaking out. They weren't weeping and fasting.

> The heroes of the faith weren't hunting down God's will. God's will came out of nowhere and found them.

God's will can find us wherever we are. As long we are trusting Him, serving Him, and willing to follow Him wherever He calls us.

What if I fail?

It's the question that keeps us awake at night. It's what keeps us from pursuing our dreams. We are terrified of failure.

Recently, I was reminded of something that changed my whole perspective on failure.

I was enjoying a Caesar salad and some Central California sun with an old friend. I sat across the table from a woman who'd watched me grow up. She asked about my life and my current plans. I told her all about my books and hopes and dreams, spilling my heart the way only good friends can. I confessed a few of my worries. Then she smiled at me and said something that changed the way I viewed my future:

"What have you got to lose?"

I blinked. *Nothing.* I have nothing to lose.

And neither do you. Because, sister, we serve the same God. In Him, we have nothing to lose and nothing to fear.

Winston Churchill said, "Success is not final. Failure is not fatal. It is the courage to continue that counts."

There is only one kind of person who never fails,
and that is the person who never tries.

If we step out and chase God's dreams for us, we are all going to fail at some point. All of us have to come to the end of ourselves some time. But I would so much rather fail while daring greatly than never try at all.

The answer to finding God's will for our lives is also the greatest commandment.

You shall love the Lord your God with all your heart,
With all your soul, and with all your strength.

Deuteronomy 6:5

If you are in His Word, serving Him, loving Him, willing to follow Him, He will find you. I promise. I guarantee it. God always shows up when His children ask.

And when He shows up, when He gives you that dream for your life, pray through it, make sure it lines up with Scripture, and confirm it with godly authority.

Then you go for it. Follow the Lord wherever He goes and don't you dare look back.

He has given you all you need to live an exceptional life for His glory. You are more than equipped to run this race of faith dauntlessly and conquer every fear that stands between you and your destiny. You are God's game-changer, beloved. You are His message to this earth.

May we never be numbered with the cold and timid souls who know neither victory nor defeat.

Forget the critics.

Eyes on your Savior.

Charge forward in faith.

Because you and I weren't born for normal lives.

Beautiful girl, you were born to dare greatly.

CHAPTER 10

DARE GREATLY

DAILY STUDY GUIDE

DAY 1
Read Psalm 37:4-6

What three commands are in this passage?

What are we promised in return for obeying these commands?

What are practical ways we can delight ourselves in the Lord?

HANNAH DUGGAN

Do you know what you'd like to do with your life? If so, what?

Lucky for us, knowing what we're doing with our life isn't a requirement for receiving God's direction. We're simply told to commit our way to Him and trust that He will bring it pass. Whether you know what you want to do with your life or not, commit your way to Him right now. Hand over your future. Trust also in Him, and He will bring it to pass. Lift up your life to Him in a prayer below.

DAY 2
Read Luke 5:1-11

What did Jesus tell Peter to do?

What was Peter's response?

When he saw what Jesus did, how did Peter's reaction change?

What is the last thing said about the fishermen on that boat?

One more reason to love our God. Here's the Lord of the Universe. He could have moved mountains, quite literally, to prove His Godhood. Instead, what does he do? He uses fishing, something near and dear to Peter's heart, to prove that He is God. Has the Lord ever revealed Himself to you in a practical, hands-on way? What happened?

This isn't the first time Peter and Jesus had met. Just one chapter earlier, Jesus had healed his mother-in-law. He'd already seen Jesus work miracles, but this one hit home. I believe that it was right then that Peter realized exactly Who he was dealing with. When did you come face to face with Jesus and realize Who you were dealing with?

DAY 3
Read John 1:43-51

What was Nathaniel's initial response to the news of the Messiah?

What was the first thing Jesus said to him?

What convinced Nathaniel of Who Jesus was?

Nathaniel was the critic, the skeptic, and—from what we see here—the guy who always said exactly what he was thinking. Jesus knew everything about Nathaniel. He could have said, "Behold, an Israelite in whom there nothing but cynicism." Instead, He pointed out Nathaniel's best quality. But it's not the compliment that convinces Nathaniel. It's what Jesus says next. To us, the fig tree thing might not make sense, but in that day "under the fig tree" was a figure of speech that meant to study the Scriptures. Most scholars believe that Nathaniel had been reading the Jewish Scriptures and God had spoken to him. It was such an important moment in Nathaniel's life, just him and God. Then here comes this prophet who says, "I know you, Nathaniel, because I was there with you, under the fig tree." Have you ever had a personal, "fig tree" moment with God when it was just the two of you? Explain.

Sometimes we're waiting for God's will to come in the "lightning from Heaven" moments. Sometimes it comes in the quiet moments when we're worshiping God. Spend time simply worshiping Him. Try to have a prayer time solely devoted to worship. I dare you to be thankful and focus on Jesus the whole time and not to ask for anything. Record your praise below.

Day 4
Read Micah 6:6-8

What does Micah want to offer the Lord?

What three things does the Lord require of us?

Micah was an Old Testament prophet and a contemporary of Isaiah. Israel had fallen into a period of rebellion during this time. While they were sacrificing their own children to idols, they were still trying to look holy. Micah is condemning their attitude with these verses, saying that we can never atone for all the wrong we've done, but God never asked us to. Here, more than seven-hundred years before the birth of Jesus, Micah was grappling with the concept of grace. It's easy for us to judge the Israelites for their attitude, but we do the same thing today. We think that if we give God control of our life, He's going to ask us to do something horrible, something we'll hate. What are you most afraid God will call you to do?

Our God loves to call us out of our comfort zones, but at the same time, His yoke is easy and burden is light (Matt. 11:28). He is not calling you to something that you can't bear. So often, we think that in order to please Him, we have to make ourselves miserable, but that's not how our God works. He desires that we would seek justice, love mercy, and walk humbly with Him. If we're doing that, He's going to show us His will for our lives. In an earlier chapter of homework, I asked you what you would do if God let you choose anything. Turn back to your homework from Chapter 8, Day 3, and look at your answer. Your tenth and final dare is to search out God's will for your future. Below, pray over your dream. Pray that if it's God's will for you, He will show you how to move forward, and pray that if it's not His will, He'll take the desire from your heart and give you a new one.

DAY 5
Read Deuteronomy 6:4-12

How are we to love the Lord our God?

When was Israel to remember this?

What is God's warning to them?

This passage is known as the Shema. It was often the first Scripture that Jewish children learned. Israel took these instructions very literally. Not only did they teach these verses to their children, but some of the priests even wore a box called a tefillin strapped to their forehead containing these verses. Jesus listed this verse as the greatest commandment (Mark 12:30). God gave this instruction to Israel at a very pivotal time. They were standing on the border of the Promised Land. Just beyond the Jordan River lay their future and everything God had promised them. It wasn't going to be easy. There were going to be uphill battles against giants. Like Israel, in our teens we stand on the border of adulthood looking in, hoping that God will come through for us. In your opinion, what is the scariest thing about becoming an adult?

Notice that as Israel stood on the border of the Promised Land, God didn't say, "If you have enough faith the land will be yours." The land already was theirs. We get the wrong idea. We think that faith is some emotion we have to work up, but if that was true, we'd see God giving Israel a pep-talk. Instead, He tells them to make God's Word the most important part of their lives. Because "faith comes by hearing and hearing by the Word of God," (Rom. 10:17). So many of the things we've talked about in this study do take practice. They aren't easy, but they *are* already ours. Sometimes we need to beat down some giants in order to live in the peace and the joy God has prepared for us. But make no mistake, sister, the exceptional life we've talked about *is* possible. What would you say has impacted you the most in this study?

There is a mixture of sadness and joy at the end of every season. Deuteronomy is a great example. While the children of Israel were entering the bountiful Land of Promise, they were also leaving behind the safe life they had known. As we stand on the shores of the Jordan together, I am so proud of you. You made it all the way! Our ten-week journey might be over, but, girl, we've got a long way to go. So I leave you with a final Greek word. It just so happens to be my favorite. At the end of all things, God will declare, "It is done!" (Rev. 21:6). The word for "done" is *ginomai*. Oddly enough, that word means "to come into existence." It's the same word used for when Jesus *turned* the water into wine. It literally means to take something and turn it into something else. *Ginomai* is a beginning wrought from an end. This is the end of our study, but, dear one, you and I know it is just the beginning. May God seal these lessons in our hearts and *ginomai* them into something beautiful and eternal.

Grace and peace to you.

IF YOU DON'T KNOW JESUS

Dare Greatly is designed to build you in your faith and encourage you as you walk with God, but I know that some of you who are reading it do not know Jesus Christ as your personal Savior. I know this because I have prayed for you, prayed that God would put this book in your hands so that you can find out Who He is.

This Bible study is full of advice, tips, and ideas that help us to live godly lives, but you know what? They are all pointless if Jesus Christ is not the Lord of your life. Without Him it doesn't matter, because without Him we can't find our true identity, we can't possess true joy, and we can't truly live out our destiny. It doesn't matter how good we are. We've all fallen short of God's glory (Romans 3:23). We all need forgiveness.

I don't know where you're coming from. Maybe you've never set foot in church. Maybe church is your life. Maybe you are desperate to find faith. Maybe you're a church kid who's wondering if you really believe this thing. Whoever you are I want you to know that Jesus Christ loves you with an everlasting love.

No matter who you are.

No matter what you've done.

No matter who has hurt you in the past.

No matter how many times you've heard it.

He loves you. He took special care as He created you. He's watched you as you've struggled and stumbled. He holds your every tear in the palm of His hand. He thought of you with His dying breath.

He doesn't want us to handle life on our own. We can't do this without Him, and He knows that. Faith is all about letting go and putting our hope in a God Who has promised to catch us.

Nothing else in life will ever fulfill us, not money, not fame, and not romance. He is everything we long for.

If you would like to give your life to Jesus Christ today, just tell Him. Not sure what to say? This is something called the sinner's prayer. These aren't magic words. They simply cover the basics.

Dear Jesus,

I know that I'm a sinner. I've made mistakes. I know that I don't deserve to go to Heaven, and that nothing I could ever do could make me worthy. I believe that you are God. I believe that You died to pay for my sins, and I believe that You came back from the dead. Thank You for loving me. Do whatever You want with my life. It's Yours now.
In Jesus Name, Amen.

I so wish I could be there with you. I wish I could pray with you, but I want to hear your story. I want to know if you prayed that prayer. We are sisters in Christ now, and I am so excited to welcome you into this family! Please send me an email at authorhannahduggan@gmail.com.

Let me rejoice with you.
I love you dearly!

ACKNOWLEDGMENTS

Special thanks to my parents who have always supported me in my pursuits. My big ideas, crazy ideas, and silly ideas have always been so lovingly maintained by your belief in me. Thank you for teaching me what it means to dare greatly.

To Darien Gee for mentoring me and always having new ideas for me to tackle. Thank you so much for guiding my steps and showing me how wide my horizons can be.

To my girls, Peyton, Caitlin, Olivia, Tierney, and Tatyana. You are my comfort and my joy! Thank you for inspiring me, encouraging me, and reading everything I throw at you. I adore you guys.

To my beta readers, Elizabeth, Peyton, Olivia, Claire, Eva, and Tierney for reading my manuscript in a hurry and giving me the feedback I needed to get through the editing process.

To the girls' groups in California, Michigan, Texas, and Hawaii submitted ideas for this Bible study.

To all of the girls who have written me and shared their stories. You are the reason for this book. You inspire me endlessly. Keep changing the world.

To my Lord and Savior, who breathes His dreams into my heart, catches me when I fall, and forgives me when I fail. To You be all the glory. Amen.

Scripture References

Chapter 1: Live Exceptionally
Scriptures:
Jeremiah 1:7
Jeremiah 29:11
John 10:10

Chapter 2: Wait Patiently
Scriptures:
Lamentations 3:26
1 Thessalonians 4:3
2 Corinthians 6:14
1 Peter 5:5
Hebrews 13:5

Chapter 3: Conquer Courageously
Scriptures:
1 John 4:18
Psalm 23:1-6
Matthew 6:31
John 16:33
Psalm 103:8
Deuteronomy 28:2

Chapter 4: Adorn Valiantly
Scriptures:
Proverbs 31:29-30
Proverbs 31:10-28
1 Corinthians 8:9

Chapter 5: Run Dauntlessly
Scriptures:
1 Corinthians 9:24
Hebrews 12:1
Hebrews 11:32-34
Romans 8:18
2 Corinthians 4:7

Chapter 6: Fight Relentlessly
Scriptures:
2 Corinthians 10:3-5
Ephesians 6:12

Chapter 7: Transform Endlessly
2 Corinthians 5:17
Galatians 5:17
Matthew 5:30
Romans 12:2
Philippians 1:6

Chapter 8: Go Boldly
Scriptures:
Acts 1:8
Ephesians 4:11-12
1 Corinthians 3:6-7
Matthew 7:11
Luke 10:2

Chapter 9: Walk Confidently
Scriptures:
Psalm 37:1-3
1 Samuel 17:28-36
1 Peter 3:15
Matthew 13:55, 57
James 4:7

Chapter 10: Dare Greatly
Scriptures:
Jeremiah 29:11-13
Deuteronomy 30:11, 14
Psalm 37:4
Exodus 3:1-2
1 Kings 19:19
Matthew 4:18-19
Deuteronomy 6:5

About the Author

Hannah Duggan is the author of several works, both fiction and non-fiction. As a Bible teacher, dance instructor, and youth leader, she spends her time investing in the lives of girls all around her. When she's not writing or teaching girls' retreats, she is serving at her church, Calvary Chapel Hamakua and spending time with her parents and two younger brothers.

To learn more about Hannah, her books, or her ministry visit www.authorhannahduggan.wordpress.com

To get in touch with her or find out how she can connect with your girls' group, write her at authorhannahduggan@gmail.com

JUST US GIRLS:
A Bible Study on Being God's Girl in Middle School

Middle school isn't easy. It's when you're figuring out who you are, who you hang out with, and what you believe. It's when friends become enemies and boys become...cute. It's obvious we need some girl time. I'll bring the discussion. You bring the chocolate. We all need a day now and then when it's *Just Us Girls*. Life gets tough. People get mean. How do we push through? What does God's plan mean for our lives? What does it mean to be God's girl in middle school? Well, that's what Just Us Girls is all about. Together we're going to search the Word of God and find out:

- who you were meant to be
- what to do about drama
- where to find a good friend
- how beautiful you really are
- why God picked you to change the world

Made in the USA
Columbia, SC
20 December 2017